You Can

Heal Your Life

Companion Book

Also by Louise L. Hay

All of the above are available at your local bookstore, or may be ordered by visiting:
Hay House USA: **www.hayhouse.com**®;
Hay House Australia: **www.hayhouse.com.au**;
Hay House UK: **www.hayhouse.co.uk**; Hay House South Africa: **orders@psdprom.co.za**;
Hay House India: **www.hayhouseindia.co.in**

Louise's Websites: **www.LouiseHay.com**
or **www.LouiseLHay.com**

All of the above can be ordered through your local bookstore, or call or fax:
(800) 654-5126 • (800) 650-5115 (fax)
Please visit the Hay House Website at: **www.hayhouse.com**

You Can Heal Your Life Companion Book

Louise L. Hay

HAY HOUSE, INC.
Carlsbad, California
London • Sydney • Johannesburg
Vancouver • Hong Kong • New Delhi

Published and distributed in the United States by: Hay House, Inc.: www.hayhouse.com
• *Published and distributed in Australia by:* Hay House Australia Pty. Ltd.:
www.hayhouse.com.au • *Published and distributed in the United Kingdom by:* Hay
House UK, Ltd.: www.hayhouse.co.uk • *Published and distributed in the Republic of
South Africa by:* Hay House SA (Pty), Ltd.: orders@psdprom.co.za • *Distributed in
Canada by:* Raincoast: www.raincoast.com • *Published in India by:* Hay House
Publications (India) Pvt. Ltd.: www.hayhouseindia.co.in

Editorial supervision: Jill Kramer   •   *Design:* Summer McStravick

Portions of this book were originally published as part of the
Love Yourself, Heal Your Life Workbook, by Louise L. Hay, © 1990, Hay House, Inc.

ISBN 13: 978-1-56170-878-9
ISBN 10: 1-56170-878-X

09   08   07   06   6   5   4   3
1st printing, January 2002
3rd printing, August 2006

Printed in China

Dedication

I call this a companion book to *You Can Heal Your Life*. *Workbook* is such a strong word, and many of us feel that hard work is exactly what we must do in order to eradicate old, embedded thought patterns. I don't believe that making inner changes has to be "work," or difficult or painful either. I believe that it can be an adventure.

So, I would like to dedicate this book to the adventurer in *you*. You are on a treasure hunt. Each old, negative pattern that you discover is only something to be examined and released. Beneath each pattern is a storehouse of treasure within.

Seek your own gold. Create your own good health. Fill your life with love. Find your own freedom. You are worthy. You do deserve. I will help you.

You are on a pathway to inner enlightenment. As you free yourself, you also help to heal the planet.

Contents

Part I
Introduction

Part II
The Process

Part III
Your New Life

Part I

INTRODUCTION

BASIC TECHNIQUES

"I am willing to change."

This is a book about change. I know—you want everybody and everything *else* to change. Your mother, father, boss, friend, sister, lover, landlord, neighbor, minister, or government official must change so that your life can be perfect. It doesn't work that way. If you want change in your life, then *you* are the one who must do the changing. When you change, then all the other people in your world will change in relation to you.

Are you willing to change?

If you *are* willing, then you can create the life you say you want. All you have to do is change some thoughts and release some beliefs. Sound simple? It is. However, it's not always easy. We will explore some of the things you may have beliefs about in different areas of your life. If you have positive beliefs, then I urge you to keep them and expand upon them. If you find negative beliefs, then I'll help you let them go.

My life is a good example of what can happen when you change your thinking. I went from being a battered and abused child who grew up in poverty, with little self-esteem and many problems, to a well-known woman who's able to help others. I no longer live in pain and suffering. I've created a wonderful life for myself. You can do it, too.

I encourage you to be gentle with yourself as you embark on the exercises in this book. And yet, even if you can only do one exercise per month, it will still be helpful. Do what you can. The exercises will give you new information about yourself. You will be able to make new choices. Every new choice you make is like planting a seed in your new mental garden. The seeds may take time to germinate and grow. Remember, when you plant a seed, you don't produce an instant apple tree. Similarly, you may not always get instant results from doing this work.

I advise you to use this companion book in sections. Try to do a segment of your life at a time. Really examine your feelings as you do each exercise. Read through the book once. Allow thoughts and memories to come up. Then go back and do all the exercises even if you have no problems in that area. You may be surprised by what comes up. Do the exercises several times if there's an area of difficulty for you. Create exercises of your own.

Sometimes it's good to have a box of tissues nearby. Give yourself permission to explore the past, and cry if necessary. Tears are the river of life and are very cleansing.

I would like to review the basic beliefs that support my philosophy. You may remember them from *You Can Heal Your Life*.

What I Believe

Life is very simple. What we give out, we get back. I believe that everyone, myself included, is responsible for every experience in our lives, the best and the worst. Every thought we think is creating our future. Each one of us creates our experiences by the thoughts we think and the words we speak and the beliefs we hold.

Beliefs are ideas and thoughts that we accept as truth. What we think about ourselves and the world becomes true for us. What we choose to believe can expand and enrich our world. Each day can be an exciting, joyous, hopeful experience; or a sorrowful, limiting, and painful one. Two people living in the same world, with the same set of circumstances, can experience life so differently. What can transport us from one world to another? I'm convinced that it's our beliefs that do so. When we're willing to change our primary belief structures, then we may experience a true change in our lives.

Whatever your beliefs may be about yourself and the world, remember that they're only thoughts, and thoughts can be changed. You may not agree with some of the ideas that I'm about to explore. Some of them may be unfamiliar and frightening. Don't worry. Only those ideas that are right for you will become part of you. You may think that some of the techniques are too simple or foolish and could not possibly work for you. I'm only asking you to try them.

Our subconscious mind accepts whatever we choose to believe. The Universal Power never judges or criticizes us. It only accepts us at our own value. If you accept a limiting belief, then it will become the truth for you. If you believe that you're too short, too fat, too thin, too tall, too smart, not smart enough, too rich, too poor, or incapable of forming relation-ships, then those beliefs will become true for you.

Remember that we're dealing with thoughts, and thoughts can be changed. We have unlimited choices about what we can think, and the point of power is always in the present moment.

What are you thinking in the present moment? Is it pos-itive or negative? Do you want this thought to be creating your future?

When we were children, we learned about life and about our-selves from the reactions of the adults around us. Therefore, most of us have ideas about who we are that were merely someone else's opinions. And we have many rules about how life "should" be lived. If you lived with people who were un-happy, frightened, guilty, or angry, then you learned a lot of negative things about yourself and your world.

When we grow up, we have a tendency to re-create the emo-tional environment of our early home life. We also tend to re-create in our personal relationships the ones we had with our mother and father. If we were highly criticized or abused as chil-dren, then we will seek out those individuals in our adult life who will duplicate this behavior. If we were praised, loved, and encouraged as children, then we will re-create those patterns.

I do not encourage you to blame your parents. We are all victims of victims, and they couldn't teach you something that they didn't know. If your mother or father didn't know how to love themselves, it would have been impossible for them to teach *you* how to love yourself. They were coping as best they could with the information they had. Think for a minute about how they were raised. If you want to understand your parents more, I suggest that you ask them about their childhoods.

Listen to not only *what* they're telling you, but notice what happens to them *while* they're speaking. What is their body language like? Can they make eye contact with you? Look into their eyes and see if you can find their inner child. You may only see it for a split second, but it may reveal some valuable information.

I believe that we choose our parents. I believe that we've decided to incarnate on this earth in a particular time and space. We've come here to learn specific lessons that will advance us on our spiritual, evolutionary pathway. I believe that we choose our sex, color, and country, and then we search for the particular set of parents who will enhance our spiritual work in this lifetime.

All that we're dealing with is a thought, and a thought can be changed. No matter what the problem is, your experiences are outer effects of inner thoughts. Even self-hatred is only a thought you have about yourself. This thought produces a feeling, and you buy into that feeling. However, if you don't have the thought, you won't have the feeling. Thoughts can be changed. Change the thought, and the feeling most go.

The past has no power over us. It doesn't matter how long we've been in a negative pattern. We can be free in this moment.

Believe it or not, we do choose our thoughts. We may habitually think the same thought over and over so that it doesn't seem as if we're choosing the thought. But we did make the original choice. We can refuse to think certain thoughts. How often have you refused to think a positive thought about yourself? You can also refuse to think a negative thought about yourself.

The innermost belief for everyone I've worked with is always, "I'm not good enough!" Everyone I know or have worked with is suffering from self-hatred or guilt to one degree or another. "I'm not good enough, I don't do enough, or I don't deserve this," are common complaints. But for whom are you not good enough? And by whose standards?

I find that resentment, criticism, guilt, and fear cause most of the problems in ourselves and in our lives. These feelings come from blaming others and not taking responsibility for our own experiences. If we're all responsible for everything in our lives, then there's no one to blame. Whatever is happening "out there" is only a mirror of our own inner thinking.

I do not condone other people's poor behavior, but it's our own belief system that attracts this behavior to us. There's some thought in you that attracts people who exhibit abusive behavior. If you find that people are constantly mistreating you, then this is your belief pattern. When you change the thought that attracts this behavior, it will stop.

We can change our attitudes toward the past. It's over and done and can't be changed. Yet we *can* change our thoughts about the past. How foolish for us to punish ourselves in the present moment because someone hurt us long ago.

If we choose to believe that we're helpless victims and that it's all hopeless, then the Universe will support us in that belief. Our worst opinions of ourselves will be confirmed.

If we choose to believe that we're responsible for our experiences, the good and the so-called bad, then we have the opportunity to outgrow the effects of the past. We can change. We can be free.

The road to freedom is through the doorway to forgiveness. We may not know how to forgive, and we may not *want* to forgive; but if we're *willing* to forgive, we may begin the healing process. It's imperative for our own healing that we release the past and forgive everyone.

I'm not saying that it's all right that someone behaved in a misguided way. However, we must be aware that the past is over. We only carry the hurt and the memory in our mind. This is what we want to let go of—the pain we're continuing to cause ourselves because we won't forgive. Forgiveness means giving up, letting go. We understand our own pain so well, yet it's hard for most of us to understand the pain of someone who treated us badly. That person we need to forgive was also in pain. And they're only mirroring what *we* believed about ourselves. They were doing the best they could, given the knowledge, understanding, and awareness they possessed at the time.

When people come to me with a problem—I don't care what it is—poor health, lack of money, unfulfilling relationships, or stifled creativity—there's only one thing that I ever work on, and that is *loving the self*.

I find that when we really love, accept, and approve of ourselves exactly as we are, everything in life flows. Joyous self-approval and self-acceptance in the here and now are the keys to positive change in every area of our lives.

To me, loving the self means never, ever criticizing ourselves for anything. Criticism locks us into the very pattern we're trying to change.

Try approving of yourself and see what happens. You've been criticizing yourself for years. Has it worked?

COMPANION BOOK TERMINOLOGY

Affirmations

We'll be using affirmations throughout this book. Affirmations are any statements that we make—either positive or negative. In fact, every word we speak and every thought we think is an affirmation. When we talk about *doing* affirmations, we mean making conscious positive statements to improve the quality of our lives. Too often we think in terms of negative affirmations, which only create more of what we don't want. Saying, "I hate this old car" will get us nowhere. Declaring, "I bless my old car and release it with love; I now accept and deserve a beautiful new car" will begin to open the channels in our consciousness to create that effect.

Make positive statements about how you want your life to be. One important point is: *Always make your statements in the PRESENT TENSE*, such as "I am" or "I have." Your subconscious mind is such an obedient servant that if you make a declaration in the future tense, such as "I want," or "I will have," then that's where your desire will always stay—just out of your reach.

Dr. Bernie Siegel, bestselling author of *Love, Medicine & Miracles*, says that "affirmations are not a denial of the present, but a hope for the future. As you allow them to permeate your consciousness, they will become more and more believable until eventually they may become real for you."

Mirror Work

Mirror work is another valuable tool. Mirrors reflect the feelings we have about ourselves. They clearly show us the areas that need to be changed if we want a joyous, feeling life.

I ask people to look in their own eyes and say something positive about themselves every time they pass a mirror. The most powerful way to do your affirmations is to look in the mirror and say them out loud. You're immediately aware of any resistance and can move through it quicker.

Keep a hand mirror near you as you read this book. Use a larger mirror for some of the deeper exercises.

Visualization

Visualization is the process of using the imagination to achieve a desired result. Put most simply, you see what you want to happen before it actually does happen. Some people say they can't visualize. Then I ask them to describe their bathroom. As they do, I tell them, "This is visualization."

For example, if what you desire is a new place to live, picture a house or apartment that you want, being as specific as possible. Then see it as if it were already a reality. Affirm that you deserve it. See your new home with you in it, going about your daily routine. Picture this scenario as clearly as you can, knowing that there's no wrong way to visualize. Practice your visualization frequently, turning all results over to the Universal Mind, and asking for your highest good. Combined with positive affirmations, visualization is a most powerful tool.

Deservability

Sometimes we refuse to put any effort into creating a good life for ourselves because we believe that we don't deserve it. The belief that we aren't deserving usually comes from our early childhood experiences. Maybe the belief came from our early toilet training. Perhaps we were told that we couldn't have what we wanted if we didn't eat all of our food, clean our room, or put our toys away. Or maybe we were subjected to abuse. We could be buying into another person's concept or opinion that has nothing to do with our own reality.

Deserving has everything to do with having good in our lives. It's our unwillingness to *accept* that gets in the way. Allow yourself to accept good, whether you think you deserve it or not.

EXERCISE: DESERVABILITY

Answer the following questions as best you can. They will help you understand the power of deservability.

1. **What do you want that you do not have now? Be clear and specific about your desires.**

_____

_____

_____

_____

_____

_____

2. **What were the laws/rules in your home about deserving? Did they tell you that "you don't deserve" or "you deserve a good smack"? Did your parents feel deserving? Did you always have to earn in order to deserve? Did earning work for you? Were you told that you were no good? Or that sinners don't deserve? Were things taken away from you when you did something wrong?**

_____

_____

_____

_____

_____

_____

_____

3. Do you feel that you deserve? What is the thought that
    comes up: "Later, when I earn it" or "I have to work
    for it first"? Are you good enough? Will you ever be good
    enough?

_____

_____

_____

_____

_____

_____

4. Do you deserve to live? Why? Why not? Were you ever told, "You deserve to die"? If so, was this part of your religious upbringing?

_____

_____

_____

_____

_____

_____

5. What do you have to live for? What is the purpose in your life? What meaning have you created? Are you filled with joy when you awaken?

_____

_____

_____

_____

_____

_____

6. Whom do you need to forgive in order to deserve? Bitterness puts a wall around our heart and makes it difficult for us to receive.

_____

_____

_____

_____

_____

_____

7. What do you deserve? Do you believe: "I deserve love and joy and all good"? Or do you feel deep down that you deserve nothing? Why? Where did the message come from? Are you willing to let it go? What are you willing to put in its place? Remember, these are thoughts, and thoughts can be changed.

_____

_____

_____

_____

_____

_____

You can see that personal power is affected by the way we perceive our deservability. Try this next treatment. Put most simply, treatments are positive statements made in any given situation to establish new thought patterns and dissolve old ones.

Deservability Treatment

I am one with Life, and all of Life loves and supports me.
I am deserving. I deserve all good. Not some, not a little bit,
but all good. I now move past all negative, restricting thoughts.
I release and let go of the limitations of my parents. I can
love them, and I can go beyond them. I am not their negative
opinions nor their limiting beliefs. I am not bound by any
of the fears or prejudices of the current society I live in.
I no longer identify with limitation of any kind.
In my mind, I have total freedom. I now move into a new
space of consciousness where I am willing to see myself
differently. I am willing to create new thoughts about myself
and about my life. My new thinking becomes new experiences.
I now know and affirm that I am at one with the Prospering
Power of the Universe. As such, I now prosper in a number
of ways. The totality of possibilities lies before me. I deserve
a good life. I deserve an abundance of love. I deserve good
health. I deserve to live comfortably and to prosper. I deserve
joy and happiness. I deserve freedom to be all that I can be.
I deserve more than that. I deserve all good.
The Universe is more than willing to manifest my new
beliefs. This is the truth of my being, and I accept it as so.
All is well in my world.

I approve of myself
The point of power is always in the present
I am responsible for my experiences
My thoughts create my future

Chapter Two

BELIEFS

"I see myself with eyes of love, and I am safe."

In this chapter, I would like us to look at ourselves and our beliefs. We all have many positive things we believe, and we want to continue to reinforce these beliefs. However, many of our beliefs are negative and continue to contribute to uncomfortable experiences. It's impossible for us to change any limiting beliefs unless we know what they are.

Look at the list of words below. Write down any positive or negative beliefs that they bring up for you. For example, do you believe that . . .

Men . . .

. . . are superior	or	. . . are supportive
. . . are bossy	or	. . . are loving
. . . leave you	or	. . . honor and respect you

Women . . .

. . . get paid less	or	. . . are powerful
. . . have to do all the housework	or	. . . deserve success
. . . have to obey men	or	. . . are a joy to be around

Love . . .

. . . is not for you	or	. . . is what you deserve
. . . has passed you by	or	. . . can happen at any time
. . . equates to loss and heartbreak	or	. . . is a wonderful part of life

Sex . . .

. . . is dirty	or	. . . is natural and healthy
. . . is only for marriage	or	. . . is a gift two people share
. . . is painful and scary	or	. . . is a pleasurable experience

Work . . .

. . . is boring	or	. . . is fulfilling and meaningful
. . . is an unpleasant necessity	or	. . . is enjoyable every day
. . . is financially unsatisfying	or	. . . pays you what you believe you deserve

Money . . .

... is always in   or   ... is available in abundance
short supply

... is something to fear   or   ... helps you live a
pleasurable life

... leads to debt   or   ... provides security

Success . . .

... is a goal you'll   or   ... is your birthright
never attain

... is only for the rich   or   ... is possible for everyone

... is for others,   or   ... is part of your life
not you   right now

Failure . . .

... is unacceptable   or   ... is something you forgive
yourself for

... means doing   or   ... is a normal part of life
it wrong

... is what you expect   or   ... can be a learning
experience

God . . .

... is out to get you   or   ... loves you always
for your sins

... is Someone to fear   or   ... accepts and forgives you

... disapproves of you   or   ... supports your efforts

Now it's your turn. Think of all the beliefs that these words bring to mind for you. Add other areas of your life that are not working well. Make the list as long as you like. Write everything down—both your positive and negative beliefs—so you can see your thoughts clearly. These are the internal, subconscious rules you live your life by. You cannot make positive changes in your life until you can recognize the beliefs you hold.

Men . . .

_____

_____

_____

_____

_____

_____

_____

Women . . .

_____

_____

_____

_____

_____

_____

_____

Love . . .

_____

_____

_____

_____

_____

_____

_____

Sex . . .

_____

_____

_____

_____

_____

_____

Work . . .

_____

_____

_____

_____

_____

_____

Money . . .

_____

_____

_____

_____

_____

_____

_____

Success . . .

_____

_____

_____

_____

_____

_____

_____

Failure . . .

_____

_____

_____

_____

_____

_____

_____

God . . .

_____

_____

_____

_____

_____

_____

_____

When the list is more or less complete, read it over. Place an asterisk (*) next to each belief that is nourishing and supportive of you. These beliefs are the ones you want to keep and reinforce. Place a check (✓) next to each belief that is negative and detrimental to your goals. These are the beliefs that are holding you back from being all that you can be. These are the beliefs you want to erase, drop, or reprogram.

Now, notice the areas that are difficult for you. Do you have conflicting beliefs? How many of your answers are negative? Do you really want to continue to build your life on these convictions? Be aware that someone taught you these ideas. Now that you've seen them, you can choose to let them go.

We're not looking at what's *wrong* with us; we're looking at the barriers that we've put up that keep us from realizing our potential. And without self-bashing, we eliminate these barriers and beliefs and make positive changes. Yes, many of those barriers are things we learned in childhood. If we learned them once, then we can now unlearn them.

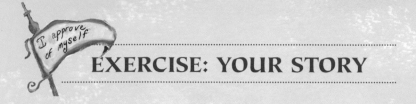

EXERCISE: YOUR STORY

This would be a good time for you to write a brief story of your life. Begin with your childhood. Use more paper if you need to.

_____

_____

_____

_____

_____

_____

_____

_____

_____

_____

What other negative beliefs could you have rattling around in your subconscious mind? Allow them to come up. You may be surprised by what you find. How many negative messages did you notice when you wrote your story? Treat each negative belief that surfaces as a treasure. "Ah-ha! I've found you. You're the one that has been causing me all this trouble. Now I can eliminate you and be free."

_____

_____

_____

_____

_____

This would be a good time to pick up your hand mirror, look in your eyes, and affirm your "willingness" to release all these old negative messages and beliefs. Breathe deeply as you do so, and speak aloud if you can: *"I am willing to release all old negative concepts and beliefs that are no longer nourishing me."* Repeat this statement several times.

The Inner Child

Many of us have an inner child who is lost and lonely and feels so rejected. Perhaps the only contact we've had with our inner child for a long time is to scold it and criticize it. Then we wonder why we're unhappy. We cannot reject a part of us and still be in harmony within. Part of healing is to gather all the parts of ourselves so that we may be whole and complete. Let's do some work to connect with these neglected inner parts of ourselves.

Find a photo—Find a photo of yourself as a child. If you don't have one, ask your parents to send you one. Study this picture closely. What do you see? It may be joy, pain, sorrow, anger, or fear. Do you love this child? Can you relate to it? (I took a small photo of myself at the age of five and had it blown up to 12" x 15" so that I could really see my "little girl.")

Write a few words about your inner child:

_____

_____

_____

_____

Draw a picture—Use several crayons, felt-tipped pens, or colored pencils. You can draw on the paper in this companion book or get a larger piece of your own. Use your non-dominant hand (the one you don't write with), and draw a picture of yourself as a child.

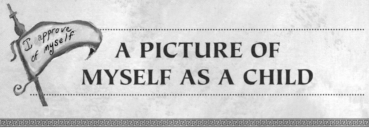

A PICTURE OF MYSELF AS A CHILD

Describe the picture—What does this picture tell you? What colors did you use? What is the child doing?

_____

_____

_____

_____

Talk to your inner child—Take a little time now to speak to your inner child. Discover more about this child. Ask it questions. Do this looking into a mirror if you can.

1.   **What do you like?**

_____

_____

_____

_____

2. What do you dislike?

_____

_____

_____

_____

3. What frightens you?

_____

_____

_____

_____

4. How do you feel?

_____

_____

_____

_____

5. What do you need?

_____

_____

_____

_____

6. How can I help you feel safe?

_____

_____

_____

_____

7. How can I make you happy?

_____

_____

_____

_____

Have a good conversation with your inner child. Be there for that child. Embrace it and love it, and do what you can to take care of its needs. Be sure to let it know that no matter what happens, you'll always be there. You *can* begin to create a happy childhood.

(Please note that this exercise works best with your eyes closed.)

Power Points

"I believe in my own power to change."

This small section may be the most important part of this book. Continually refer to it as you explore the various areas of your life. Make several lists of these seven points. Place these lists where you can see them. Read them often. Memorize them. When these concepts become part of your belief system, you'll have a different perspective on life.

POWER POINTS

1. We are each responsible for our experiences.

2. Every thought we think is creating our future.

3. Everyone is dealing with the damaging patterns of resentment, criticism, guilt, and self-hatred.

4. These are only thoughts, and thoughts can be changed.

5. We need to release the past and forgive everyone.

6. Self-approval and self-acceptance in the "now" are the keys to positive change.

7. The point of power is always in the present moment.

As you do the exercises in this companion book, keep coming back to these seven points. Don't just get stuck in your specific problems. When you really accept these ideas and make them a part of your belief system, you become "powerful," and the problems will often solve themselves. The object is to change what you believe about yourself and the world you live in.

It's not the people, places, and things that are creating a problem for you; it's how you're perceiving and creating these life experiences. Take responsibility for your own life. Don't give your power away. Learn to understand more about your inner spiritual life, and operate under that power that created only good for you.

"I give myself permission to learn."

Part II

THE PROCESS

Chapter Three

HEALTH

"I restore and maintain my body at optimum health."

Health Checklist

☐ I get three colds every year.

☐ My energy level is low.

☐ I heal slowly.

☐ My allergies act up constantly.

☐ Heart dis-ease runs in my family.

☐ I get one illness after another.

☐ My back gives me constant pain.

☐ These headaches never go away.

☐ I'm always constipated.

☐ I have sore feet.

☐ I'm always hurting my body.

Be very clear that your body is *always* trying to maintain a state of optimum health, no matter how badly you treat it. If you take good care of your body, it will reward you with vibrant health and energy.

I believe that we contribute to every "illness" in our body. The body, as with everything else in life, is a mirror of our inner thoughts and beliefs. Our body is always talking to us, if we will only take the time to listen. Every cell within our bodies responds to every single thought we think.

When we discover what the mental pattern is behind an illness, we have a chance to change the pattern and, therefore, the dis-ease. Most people don't want to be sick on a conscious level, yet every dis-ease that we have is a teacher. Illness is the body's way of telling us that there's a false idea in our consciousness. Something that we're believing, saying, doing, or thinking is not for our highest good. I always picture the body tugging at us saying, "Please—pay attention!"

Sometimes people *do* want to be sick. In our society, we've made illness a legitimate way to avoid responsibility or unpleasant situations. If we can't learn to say no, then we may have to invent a dis-ease to say no for us.

I read an interesting report a few years back. It stated that only 30 percent of patients follow their doctor's instructions. According to Dr. John Harrison, author of the fascinating book *Love Your Disease*, many people go to doctors only to have their acute symptoms relieved—so that they can *tolerate* their dis-ease. It's as if an unwritten, subconscious agreement exists between doctor and patient: The doctor agrees not to cure the patient if the patient pretends to do something about his or her condition. Also in this agreement, one person gets to pay, and the other becomes the authority figure . . . and so, both parties are satisfied.

True healing involves body, mind, and spirit. I believe that if we "cure" an illness yet do not address the emotional and spiritual issues that surround that ailment, it will only manifest again.

EXERCISE: RELEASING YOUR HEALTH PROBLEMS

Are you willing to release the need that has contributed to your health problems? Once again, when we have a condition that we want to change, the first thing that we have to do is say so. Say: *"I am willing to release the need in me that has created this condition."* Say it again. Say it looking in the mirror. Say it every time you think about your condition. It's the first step in creating a change.

1. **List all of your mother's illnesses.**

_____

_____

_____

_____

_____

2. List all of your father's illnesses.

_____

_____

_____

_____

3. List all of your illnesses.

_____

_____

_____

_____

4. Do you see a connection?

_____

_____

_____

_____

EXERCISE: HEALTH AND DIS-EASE

Let's examine some of your beliefs about health and dis-ease. Answer the following questions. Be as open and honest as you can.

1.   What do you remember about your childhood illnesses?

_____

_____

_____

_____

_____

2.   What did you learn from your parents about illness?

_____

_____

_____

_____

_____

3. What, if anything, did you enjoy about being sick as a child?

_____

_____

_____

_____

_____

4. Is there a belief about illness from your childhood that you're still acting on today?

_____

_____

_____

_____

_____

5. How have you contributed to the state of your health?

_____

_____

_____

_____

_____

6. Would you like your health to change? If so, in what way?

_____

_____

_____

_____

_____

EXERCISE: YOUR BELIEFS ABOUT SICKNESS

Complete the following statements as honestly as you can.

1.   The way I make myself sick is . . .

_____

_____

_____

_____

_____

2.   I get sick when I try to avoid . . .

_____

_____

_____

_____

_____

3. When I get sick, I always want to . . .

_____

_____

_____

_____

4. When I was sick as a child, my mother always . . .

_____

_____

_____

_____

5. My greatest fear when I'm sick is that . . .

_____

_____

_____

_____

EXERCISE: THE POWER OF AFFIRMATIONS

Let's discover the power of written affirmations! Writing an affirmation can intensify its power. In the space below, write a positive affirmation about your health 25 times. You may create your own, or use one of the following:

1. Healing is already in process.
2. I listen with love to my body's messages.
3. My health is radiant, vibrant, and dynamic now.
4. I am grateful for my perfect health.
5. I deserve good health.

1. _____

2. _____

3. _____

4. _____

5. _____

6. _____

7. _____

8. _____

9. _____

10. _____

11. _____

12. _____

13. _____

14. _____

15. _____

16. _____

17. _____

18. _____

19. _____

20. _____

21. _____

22. _____

23. _____

24. _____

25. _____

EXERCISE: SELF-WORTH

Let's examine the issue of self-worth with respect to your health. Answer the following questions, and after each one, create a positive affirmation.

1. **Do I deserve good health?**

   Sample Answer: *No. Illness runs in my family.*

   Sample Affirmation: *I accept and deserve perfect health now.*

   Your Answer:

   _____

   _____

   Your Affirmation:

   _____

   _____

2. **What do I fear most about my health?**

Sample Answer: *I'm afraid that I'll get sick and die.*

Sample Affirmation: *It is safe to be well now. I am always loved.*

Your Answer:

_____

_____

Your Affirmation:

_____

_____

3. **What am I "getting" from this belief?**

Sample Answer: *I don't have to be responsible or go to work.*

Sample Affirmation: *I am confident and secure. Life is easy for me.*

Your Answer:

_____

_____

Your Affirmation:

_____

_____

4.   What do I fear will happen if I let go of this belief?

Sample Answer: *I will have to grow up.*

Sample Affirmation: *It is safe for me to be an adult.*

Your Answer:

_____

_____

Your Affirmation:

_____

_____

⊕ ⊕ ⊕

The statements listed in the checklist at the beginning of this chapter are listed again below, along with the affirmation corresponding to each belief. Make these affirmations part of your daily routine. Say them often in the car, at work, while looking in the mirror, or any time you feel your negative beliefs surfacing.

If You Believe:	Your Affirmation Could Be:
I get three colds every year.	*I am safe and secure at all times. Love surrounds me and protects me.*
My energy level is low.	*I am filled with energy and enthusiasm.*
I heal slowly.	*My body heals rapidly.*
My allergies act up constantly.	*My world is safe. I am safe. I am at peace with all of life.*
Heart dis-ease runs in my family.	*I am not my parents. I am healthy and whole and filled with joy.*
I get one illness after another.	*Good health is mine now. I release the past.*
My back gives me constant pain.	*Life loves and supports me. I am safe.*
These headaches never go away.	*I no longer criticize myself; my mind is at peace, and all is well.*
I am always constipated.	*I allow life to flow through me.*
I have sore feet.	*I am willing to move forward with ease.*
I am always hurting my body.	*I am gentle with my body. I love myself.*

"I give myself permission to be well."

Health Treatment

I am one with Life, and all of Life loves me and

supports me. Therefore, I claim for myself perfect

vibrant health at all times. My body knows how

to be healthy, and I cooperate by feeding it healthy

foods and beverages, and exercising in ways

that are enjoyable to me. My body loves me, and

I love and cherish my precious body. I am not

my parents, nor do I choose to re-create their

illnesses. I am my own unique self, and I move

through life healthy, happy, and whole. This is

the truth of my being, and I accept it as so.

All is well in my body.

Chapter Four

FEARFUL EMOTIONS

*"Fears are merely thoughts,
and thoughts can be released."*

Fearful Emotions Checklist

☐ I'm anxious all the time.

☐ Nothing works for me.

☐ Growing older frightens me.

☐ I'm afraid of flying.

☐ People scare me.

☐ What if I become homeless?

☐ I have difficulty expressing my feelings.

☐ My temper is out of control.

☐ I can't focus on anything.

☐ Everyone is against me.

☐ I feel like a failure.

☐ What if I have to endure a painful death?

☐ I'm scared of being alone.

In any given situation, I believe that we have a choice between love and fear. We experience fear of change, fear of not changing, fear of the future, and fear of taking a chance. We fear intimacy, and we fear being alone. We fear letting people know what we need and who we are, and we fear letting go of the past.

At the other end of the spectrum, we have love. Love is the miracle we're all looking for. Loving ourselves works miracles in our lives. I'm not talking about vanity or arrogance, because that's not love. That's fear. I'm talking about having great respect for ourselves, and gratitude for the miracle of our body and mind.

Remind yourself when you're frightened that you're not loving and trusting yourself. Not feeling "good enough" interferes with the decision-making process. How can you make a good decision when you're not sure about yourself?

Susan Jeffers, in her marvelous book *Feel the Fear and Do It Anyway,* states that "if everybody feels fear when approaching something totally new in life, yet so many are out there 'doing it' despite the fear, then we must conclude that *fear is not the problem.*" She goes on to say that the real issue is not the fear, but how we *hold* the fear. We can approach it from a position of power or a position of helplessness. The fact that we have the fear becomes irrelevant.

We see what we *think* the problem is, and then we find out what the *real* problem is. Not feeling "good enough" and lacking self-love are the real problems.

Emotional problems are among the most painful of all. Occasionally we may feel angry, sad, lonely, guilty, anxious, or frightened. When these feelings take over and become predominant, our lives can become emotional battlegrounds.

What we *do* with our feelings is important. Are we going to act-out in some way? Will we punish others or force our will upon them? Will we somehow abuse ourselves?

The belief that we're *not good enough* is often at the root of these problems. Good mental health begins with *loving the self*. When we love and approve of ourselves *completely*—the good and the so-called bad—we can begin to change.

Part of self-acceptance is releasing other people's opinions. Many of the things that we've chosen to believe about ourselves have absolutely no basis in truth.

For example, a young man named Eric was a client of mine several years ago when I was seeing people privately. He was devastatingly handsome and made a good living as a model. He told me how difficult it was for him to go to the gym because he felt ugly.

As we worked together, he recalled that a neighborhood bully from his childhood used to call him "ugly." This person would also beat him up and constantly threaten him. In order to be left alone and feel safe, Eric began to hide. He bought into the fact that he wasn't good enough. In his mind, he was ugly.

Through mirror work, self-love, and positive affirmations, Eric has improved tremendously. His feelings of anxiety may come and go, but now he has some tools to work with.

Remember, feelings of inadequacy start with negative thoughts that we have about ourselves. However, these thoughts have no power over us unless we act upon them. Thoughts are only words strung together. They have *no meaning whatsoever*. Only *we* give meaning to them, and we do so by focusing on the negative messages over and over again in our minds. We believe the worst about ourselves. And *we* choose what *kind* of meaning we give to them.

Whatever pain we might be in, let's choose thoughts that nourish and support us.

We're always perfect, always beautiful, and ever-changing. We're doing the best we can with the understanding, knowledge, and awareness that we have. As we grow and change more and more, our "best" will only get better and better.

EXERCISE: LETTING GO

As you read this exercise, take a deep breath, and as you exhale, allow the tension to leave your body. Let your scalp, forehead, and face relax. Your head need not be tense in order for you to read. Let your tongue, throat, and shoulders relax. You can hold a book with relaxed arms and hands. Do that now. Let your back, abdomen, and pelvis relax. Let your breathing be at peace as you relax your legs and feet.

Can you feel a noticeable change in your body since you started reading the previous paragraph? In this relaxed, comfortable position, say to yourself, *"I am willing to let go. I release. I let go. I release all tension. I release all fear. I release all anger. I release all guilt. I release all sadness. I let go of old limitations. I let go, and I am at peace. I am at peace with myself. I am at peace with the process of life. I am safe."*

Go over this exercise two or three times. Repeat it whenever thoughts of difficulty come up. It takes a little practice for the routine to become a part of you. Once you're familiar with this exercise, you can do it anywhere, at any time. You will be able to relax completely in any situation.

EXERCISE: FEARS AND AFFIRMATIONS

After each category listed below, write down your greatest fear. Then, think of a positive affirmation that would correspond to it.

1. **CAREER**

   Sample Fear: *I'm afraid that no one will ever see my value.*

   Sample Affirmation: *Everybody at work appreciates me.*

   Your Fear:

   _____

   _____

   Your Affirmation:

   _____

   _____

2. LIVING SITUATION

Sample Fear: *I'll never have a place of my own.*

Sample Affirmation: *There is a perfect home for me, and I accept it now.*

Your Fear:

_____

_____

Your Affirmation:

_____

_____

3. FAMILY RELATIONS

Sample Fear: *My parents won't accept me the way I am.*

Sample Affirmation: *I accept my parents, and they, in turn, accept and love me.*

Your Fear:

_____

_____

Your Affirmation:

_____

_____

4. MONEY

Sample Fear: *I'm afraid of being poor.*

Sample Affirmation: *I trust that all my needs will be taken care of.*

Your Fear:

_____

_____

Your Affirmation:

_____

_____

5. PHYSICAL APPEARANCE

Sample Fear: *I think I'm fat and unattractive.*

Sample Affirmation: *I release the need to criticize my body.*

Your Fear:

_____

_____

Your Affirmation:

_____

_____

6. SEX

Sample Fear: *I'm afraid that I'll have to "perform."*

Sample Affirmation: *I am relaxed, and I flow with life easily and effortlessly.*

Your Fear:

_____

_____

Your Affirmation:

_____

_____

7. HEALTH

Sample Fear: *I'm afraid I'll get sick and won't be able to take care of myself.*

Sample Affirmation: *I'll always attract all the help I need.*

Your Fear:

_____

_____

Your Affirmation:

_____

_____

8. **RELATIONSHIPS**

Sample Fear: *I don't think anyone will ever love me.*

Sample Affirmation: *Love and acceptance are mine. I love myself.*

Your Fear:

_____

_____

Your Affirmation:

_____

_____

9. **OLD AGE**

Sample Fear: *I'm afraid of getting old.*

Sample Affirmation: *Every age has its infinite possibilities.*

Your Fear:

_____

_____

Your Affirmation:

_____

_____

10. DEATH AND DYING

Sample Fear: *What if there's no life after death?*

Sample Affirmation: *I trust the process of life. I am on an endless journey through eternity.*

Your Fear:

_____

_____

Your Affirmation:

_____

_____

EXERCISE: POSITIVE AFFIRMATIONS

Choose an area of fear from the last exercise that's most pertinent and pressing for you. Using visualization, see yourself going through the fear with a positive outcome. See yourself feeling free and being at peace.

On the lines below, write down a positive affirmation 25 times. Remember the power you're tapping into!

1. _____

2. _____

3. _____

4. _____

5. _____

6. _____

7. _____

8. _____

9. _____

10. _____

11._____

12._____

13._____

14._____

15._____

16._____

17._____

18._____

19._____

20._____

21._____

22._____

23._____

24._____

25._____

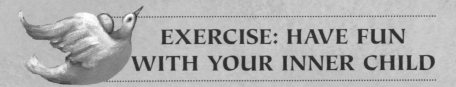

EXERCISE: HAVE FUN WITH YOUR INNER CHILD

When you're in a state of anxiety or fear that keeps you from functioning, you may have abandoned your inner child. Think of some ways in which you can reconnect with your inner child. What could you do for fun? What could you do that is *just for you*?

List 15 ways in which you could have fun with your inner child. You may enjoy reading good books, going to the movies, gardening, keeping a journal, or taking a hot bath. How about some "childlike" activities? Really take the time to think. You could run on the beach, go to a playground and swing on a swing, draw pictures with crayons, or climb a tree. Once you've made your list, try at least one activity each day. Let the healing begin!

1. _____

2. _____

3. _____

4. _____

5. _____

6. _____

7. _____

8. _____

9. _____

10. _____

11. _____

12. _____

13. _____

14. _____

15. _____

Look at all you've discovered! Keep going—you can create such fun for you and your inner child! Feel the relationship between the two of you healing.

The statements listed in the checklist at the beginning of this chapter are listed again below, along with the affirmation corresponding to each belief. Make these affirmations part of your daily routine. Say them often in the car, at work, while looking in the mirror, or any time you feel your negative beliefs surfacing.

If You Believe:	Your Affirmation Could Be:
I'm anxious all the time.	I am at peace.
Nothing works for me.	My decisions are always perfect for me.
Growing older frightens me.	My age is perfect, and I enjoy each new moment.
I'm afraid of flying.	I center myself in safety and accept the perfection of my life.
People scare me.	I am loved and safe wherever I go.
What if I become homeless?	I am at home in the Universe.
I have difficulty expressing my feelings.	It is safe to express my feelings.
My temper is out of control.	I am at peace with myself and my life.
I can't focus on anything.	My inner vision is clear and unclouded.
Everyone is against me.	I am lovable, and everybody appreciates me.
I feel like a failure.	My life is a success.
What if I have to endure a painful death?	I will die peacefully and comfortably at the right time.
I'm scared of being alone.	I express love, and I always attract love wherever I go.

"I give myself permission to be at peace."

Feeling Good Treatment

I am one with Life, and all of Life loves and supports me. Therefore, I claim for myself emotional well-being at all times. I am my best friend, and I enjoy living with myself. Experiences come and go, and people come and go, but I am always here for myself. I am not my parents, nor their patterns of emotional unhappiness. I choose to think only thoughts that are peaceful, joyous, and uplifting. I am my own unique self, and I move through life in a comfortable, safe, and peaceful way. This is the truth of my being, and I accept it as so. All is well in my heart and my mind.

Chapter Five

CRITICAL THINKING

*"I accept all my emotions,
but I do not wallow in them."*

Critical Thinking Checklist

- [ ] People are so stupid.
- [ ] I'd do it if I weren't so fat.
- [ ] Those are the ugliest clothes I've ever seen.
- [ ] They'll never be able to finish the job.
- [ ] I'm such a klutz.
- [ ] If I get angry, I'll lose control.
- [ ] I have no right to be angry.
- [ ] Anger is bad.
- [ ] When someone is angry, I get scared.
- [ ] It's not safe to be angry.
- [ ] I won't be loved if I get mad.
- [ ] Stuffing anger makes me sick.
- [ ] I've never been angry.
- [ ] My neighbors are so noisy.
- [ ] Nobody asks me what I think.

Does your internal dialogue sound like this? Is your inner voice constantly picking, picking, picking? Are you seeing the world through critical eyes? Do you judge everything? Do you stand in self-righteousness?

Most of us have such a strong tendency to judge and criticize that we can't easily break the habit. However, it's the most important issue to work on immediately. We'll never be able to really love ourselves until we go beyond the need to make life wrong.

As a little baby, you were so open to life. You looked at the world with eyes of wonder. Unless something was scary or someone harmed you, you accepted life just as it was. Later, as you grew up, you began to accept the opinions of others and make them your own.

You learned how to criticize.

EXERCISE: LETTING GO OF CRITICAL THINKING

Let's examine some of your beliefs about critical thinking. Answer the following questions. Be as open and honest as you can.

1. **What was your family pattern?**

_____

_____

_____

_____

_____

_____

_____

_____

_____

2.   What did you learn about criticism from your mother?

_____

_____

_____

_____

_____

_____

3.   What were the things she criticized?

_____

_____

_____

_____

_____

_____

4. Did she criticize you? If so, for what?

_____

_____

_____

_____

_____

_____

5. When was your father judgmental?

_____

_____

_____

_____

_____

_____

6. Did he judge himself?

_____

_____

_____

_____

_____

_____

_____

7. How did your father judge you?

_____

_____

_____

_____

_____

_____

_____

8. Was it a family pattern to criticize each other? If so, how and when did your family members do so?

_____

_____

_____

_____

_____

_____

9. When is the first time you remember being criticized?

_____

_____

_____

_____

_____

_____

10. How did your family judge your neighbors?

_____

_____

_____

_____

_____

_____

11. Did you have loving, supportive teachers at school, or were they always telling you what you were lacking? What sort of things did they tell you?

_____

_____

_____

_____

_____

12. Can you begin to see where you might have picked up
    a pattern of being critical? Who was the most critical
    person in your childhood?

_____

_____

_____

_____

_____

_____

I believe that criticism shrivels our spirits. It only enforces
the belief that "we're not good enough." It certainly doesn't
bring out the best in us.

EXERCISE: REPLACING YOUR "SHOULDS"

As I've said many times, I believe that *should* is one of the most damaging words in our language. Every time we use it, we are, in effect, saying that we *are* wrong, or we *were* wrong, or we're *going to be* wrong. I would like to take the word *should* out of our vocabulary forever and replace it with the word *could*. This word gives us a choice, and we're never wrong. Think of five things that you "should" do.

I Should:

_____

_____

_____

_____

_____

Now replace *should* with *could*.

I Could:

_____

_____

_____

_____

_____

Now, ask yourself, "Why haven't I?" You may find that you've been berating yourself for years for something that you never wanted to do in the first place, or for something that was never your idea. How many "shoulds" can you drop from your list?

EXERCISE:
MY CRITICAL SELF

Criticism breaks down the inner spirit and never changes a thing. Praise builds up the spirit and can bring about positive change. Write down two ways in which you criticize yourself in the area of love and intimacy. Perhaps you're not able to tell people how you feel or what you need. Maybe you have a fear of relationships, or you attract partners who will hurt you.

Then, think of something you can praise yourself for in this area.

Examples:

I criticize myself for: *choosing people who aren't able to give me what I need, and for being clingy in relationships.*

I praise myself for: *being able to tell someone that I like them (it scared me, yet I did it anyway); and for allowing myself to be openly loving and affectionate.*

I criticize myself for:

_____

_____

_____

_____

_____

I praise myself for:

_____

_____

_____

_____

_____

Congratulations! You've just begun to break another old habit! You're learning to praise yourself—in this moment. And the point of power is always in the present moment.

EXERCISE: ACKNOWLEDGING OUR FEELINGS

Anger is a natural and normal emotion. Babies get furious, express their fury, and then it's over. Many of us have learned that it's not nice, polite, or acceptable for us to be angry. We learn to swallow our angry feelings. They settle in our bodies, in the joints and muscles, and then they accumulate and become resentment. Layer upon layer of buried anger turned into resentment can contribute to dis-eases such as arthritis, assorted aches and pains, and even cancer.

We need to acknowledge all our emotions, including anger, and find positive ways to express these feelings. We don't have to hit people or dump on them, yet we can say simply and clearly, "This makes me angry," or "I'm angry about what you did." If it's not appropriate to say this, we still have many options: We can scream into a pillow, beat the bed, run, yell in the car with the windows rolled up, play tennis, or any number of other things. These are all healthy outlets.

1. **What was the pattern of anger in your family?**

_____

_____

_____

_____

2. What did your father do with his anger?

_____

_____

_____

_____

_____

3. What did your mother do with her anger?

_____

_____

_____

_____

_____

4. What did your brothers or sisters do with their anger?

_____

_____

_____

_____

5. Was there a family scapegoat?

_____

_____

_____

_____

_____

6. What did you do with your anger as a child?

_____

_____

_____

_____

_____

7. Did you express your anger, or did you stuff it?

_____

_____

_____

_____

_____

8. What method did you use to hold it in?

_____

_____

_____

_____

_____

9. Were you . . .

. . . an overeater?	Yes	No
. . . always sick?	Yes	No
. . . accident prone?	Yes	No
. . . getting into fights?	Yes	No
. . . a poor student?	Yes	No
. . . crying all of the time?	Yes	No

10. How do you handle your anger now?

_____

_____

_____

_____

_____

11. Do you see a family pattern?

_____

_____

_____

_____

_____

12. Which family member are you like when it comes to expressing anger?

_____

_____

_____

_____

_____

_____

13. Do you have a "right" to be angry?

_____

_____

_____

_____

_____

_____

14. Why not? Who said so?

_____

_____

_____

_____

_____

_____

15. Can you give yourself permission to express all of your feelings in appropriate ways?

_____

_____

_____

_____

_____

In order for a child to grow and blossom, it needs love, acceptance, and praise. We can be shown "better" ways to do things without making the way we do it "wrong." The child inside of you still needs that love and approval.

You can say the following positive statements to your inner child:

"I love you and know that you're doing the best you can."
"You're perfect just as you are."
"You become more wonderful every day."
"I approve of you."
"Let's see if we can find a better way to do this."
"Growing and changing is fun, and we can do it together."

These are words that children want to hear. It makes them feel good. When they feel good, they do their best. They unfold beautifully.

If your child, or your inner child, is used to constantly being "wrong," it may take a while for it to accept the new, positive words. If you make a definite decision to release criticism, and you're consistent, you can work miracles.

Give yourself one month to talk to your inner child in positive ways. Use the affirmations listed above, or make up a list of your own. Carry a list of these affirmations with you. When you notice yourself becoming judgmental, take out the list and read it two or three times. Better yet, speak it aloud in front of a mirror.

EXERCISE: LISTEN TO YOURSELF

This exercise requires a tape recorder. Tape your telephone conversations for a week or so—just your voice. When the tape is filled on both sides, sit down and listen to it. Listen to not only what you say, but the way you say it. What are your beliefs? Who and what do you criticize? Which parent, if any, do you sound like?

As you release the need to pick on yourself all the time, you'll notice that you no longer criticize others so much.

When you make it okay to be yourself, then you automatically allow others to be themselves. Their little habits no longer bother you so much. You release the need to change them. As you stop judging *others*, they release the need to judge *you*. Everybody wants to be free.

You may be a person who criticizes everyone around you. And if you do, you will certainly criticize yourself, too. So you may ask yourself:

1. **What do I get from being angry all the time?**

_____

_____

_____

_____

_____

2. What happens if I let go of my anger?

_____

_____

_____

_____

_____

_____

3. Am I willing to forgive and be free?

_____

_____

_____

_____

_____

_____

EXERCISE: WRITE A LETTER

Think of someone whom you're still angry with. Perhaps it's old anger. Write this person a letter. Tell them all your grievances and how you feel. Don't hold back. Really express yourself. Use additional paper if you need it.

_____

_____

_____

_____

_____

_____

_____

_____

_____

_____

_____

When you've finished the letter, read it once, fold it, and on the outside, write: *"What I really want is your love and approval."* Then burn the letter and release it.

Mirror Work

Think of another person, or even the same person once again, whom you're angry with. Sit down in front of a mirror. Be sure to have some tissues nearby. Look into your own eyes and "see" the other person. Tell them what you're so angry about.

When you're finished, tell them, "What I really want is your love and approval." We're all seeking love and approval. That's what we want from everyone, and that's what everyone wants from us. Love and approval bring harmony into our lives.

In order to be free, we need to release the old ties that bind us. So once again, look into the mirror and affirm to yourself, *"I am willing to release the need to be an angry person."* Notice if you're really willing to let go, or if you're holding on to the past.

The statements listed in the checklist at the beginning of this chapter are listed again below, along with the affirmation corresponding to each belief. Make these affirmations part of your daily routine. Say them often in the car, at work, while looking in the mirror, or any time you feel your negative beliefs surfacing.

If You Believe:	Your Affirmation Could Be:
People are so stupid.	*Everybody is doing the best they can, including me.*
I'd do it if I weren't so fat.	*I appreciate the wonder of my body.*
Those are the ugliest clothes I've ever seen.	*I love the uniqueness that people express in their clothing.*
They'll never be able to finish the job.	*I release the need to criticize others.*
I'm such a klutz.	*I become more proficient every day.*
If I get angry, I'll lose control.	*I express my anger in appropriate places and ways.*
I have no right to be angry.	*All of my emotions are acceptable.*
Anger is bad.	*Anger is normal and natural.*
When someone is angry, I get scared.	*I comfort my inner child, and we are safe.*
It's not safe to be angry.	*I am safe with all my emotions.*
I won't be loved if I get mad.	*The more honest I am, the more I am loved.*
Stuffing anger makes me sick.	*I allow myself freedom with all my emotions, including anger.*
I've never been angry.	*Healthy expressions of anger keep me healthy.*
My neighbors are so noisy.	*I release the need to be disturbed.*
Nobody asks me what I think.	*My opinions are valued.*

"I give myself permission to acknowledge my feelings."

Peaceful Living Treatment

I am one with Life, and all of Life loves and supports me. Therefore, I claim for myself love and acceptance on all levels. I accept all of my emotions and can express them appropriately when the occasion arises. I am not my parents, nor am I attached to their patterns of anger and judgment. I've learned to observe rather than react, and now life is much less tumultuous.

I am my own unique self, and I no longer choose to sweat the small stuff. I have peace of mind. This is the truth of my being, and I accept it as so. All is well in my inner being.

Chapter Six

ADDICTIONS

"No person, place, or thing has any power over me. I am free."

Addictions Checklist

☐ I want to relieve my pain *now*.

☐ Smoking cigarettes reduces my stress.

☐ Having lots of sex keeps me from thinking.

☐ I can't stop eating.

☐ Drinking makes me popular.

☐ I need perfection.

☐ I gamble too much.

☐ I need my tranquilizers.

☐ I can't stop buying things.

☐ I have a problem getting away from abusive relationships.

A ddictive behavior is another way of saying, "I'm not good enough." When we're caught in this type of behavior, we're trying to run away from ourselves. We don't want to be in touch with our feelings. Something that we're believing, remembering, saying, or doing is too painful for us to look at; so we overeat, drink, engage in compulsive sexual behavior, take pills, spend money that we don't have, and create abusive love relationships.

There are 12-step programs that deal with most of these addictions, and they work well for thousands of people. If you have a serious addiction problem, I encourage you to join AA or Al-Anon. They will provide you with the help you need as you go through these important changes.

In this chapter, we can't hope to duplicate the results that these programs have produced for people with addictive behavior. I believe that we must first realize that there's a need in ourselves for these compulsive actions. That need must be released before the behavior can be changed.

Loving and approving of yourself, trusting in the process of life, and feeling safe because you know the power of your own mind are extremely important issues when dealing with addictive behaviors. My experience with addicted persons has shown me that most of these individuals possess a deep self-hatred. They're very unforgiving of themselves. Day after day, they punish themselves. Why? Because somewhere along the line (most likely as children), they bought the idea that they weren't good enough—they were "bad" and in need of punishment.

Early childhood experiences that involve physical, emotional, or sexual abuse contribute to that type of self-hatred. Honesty, forgiveness, self-love, and a willingness to live in the truth can help heal these early wounds and give addictive individuals a reprieve from their behavior. I also find the addictive personality to be a fearful one. There is a great fear of letting go and trusting the process of life. As long as we believe that the world is an unsafe place with people and situations waiting to "get" us—then that belief will be our reality.

Are you willing to let go of ideas and beliefs that don't support and nurture you? If so, then you're ready to continue this journey.

EXERCISE: RELEASE YOUR ADDICTIONS

This is where the changes take place—right here and now in our own minds! Take some deep breaths; close your eyes; and think about the person, place, or thing that you're addicted to. Think of the insanity behind the addiction. You're trying to fix what you think is wrong inside of you by grabbing on to something that's outside of you. The point of power is in the present moment, and you can begin to make a shift today.

Once again, be willing to release the need. Say: *"I am willing to release the need for _____ in my life. I release it now and trust in the process of life to meet my needs."*

Say this statement every morning in your daily meditation and prayers. You've taken another step to freedom.

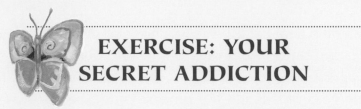

EXERCISE: YOUR SECRET ADDICTION

List ten secrets that you've never shared with anyone regarding your addiction. If you're an overeater, maybe you've eaten out of a garbage can. If you're an alcoholic, you may have kept alcohol in your car so you could drink while driving. If you're a compulsive gambler, perhaps you put your family in jeopardy in order to borrow money to feed your gambling problem. Be totally honest and open.

1. _____

2. _____

3. _____

4. _____

5. _____

6. _____

7. _____

8. _____

9. _____

10. _____

How do you feel now? Look at your "worst" secret. Visualize yourself at that period in your life, and *love* that person. Express how much you love and forgive him or her. Look into the mirror and say: "I forgive you, and I love you exactly as you are." Breathe.

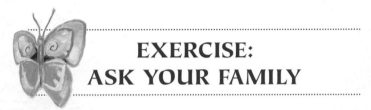

EXERCISE:
ASK YOUR FAMILY

Let's go back to our childhood for a moment and answer a few questions.

1. My mother always made me . . .

_____

_____

_____

_____

_____

_____

2. What I really wanted her to say was . . .

_____

_____

_____

_____

_____

_____

3. What my mother really didn't know was . . .

_____

_____

_____

_____

_____

_____

4. My father told me I shouldn't . . .

5. If my father only knew . . .

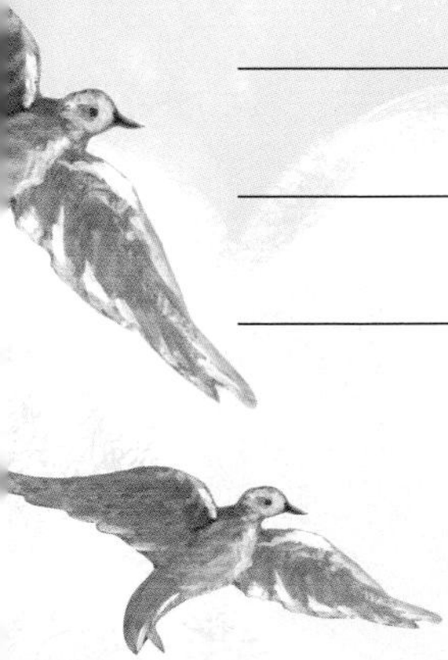

6. I wish I could have told my father . . .

_____

_____

_____

_____

_____

_____

_____

7. Mother, I forgive you for . . .

_____

_____

_____

_____

_____

_____

_____

8.   Father, I forgive you for . . .

_____

_____

_____

_____

_____

_____

Many people tell me that they can't enjoy today because of something that happened in the past. Holding on to the past *only hurts us*. We're refusing to live in the moment. The past is over and can't be changed. This is the only moment we can experience.

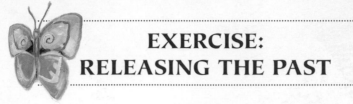

EXERCISE:
RELEASING THE PAST

Now let's clean up the past in our minds. Release the emotional attachment to it. Allow the memories to just be memories.

If you remember what you wore at the age of ten, there's usually no attachment. It's just a memory. That can be the same for *all* of the past events in our lives. As we let go, we become free to use all of our mental power to enjoy this moment and create a bright future.

We don't have to keep punishing ourselves for the past.

1. **List all of the things you're willing to let go of.**

_____

_____

_____

_____

_____

_____

2. How willing are you to let go? Notice your reactions, and write them down.

_____

_____

_____

_____

_____

_____

3. What will you have to do to let these things go? How willing are you to do so?

_____

_____

_____

_____

_____

_____

EXERCISE:
SELF-APPROVAL

Since self-hatred plays such an important role in addictive behavior, we will now do one of my favorite exercises. I've given this exercise to thousands of people, and the results are phenomenal.

Every time you think about your addiction for the next month, say over and over to yourself, "I approve of myself."

Do this three or four hundred times a day. No, it's not too many times. When you're worrying, you'll go over your problem at least that many times in a day. Let "I approve of myself" become a waking mantra, something that you say over and over to yourself, almost nonstop.

Saying this statement is guaranteed to bring up everything in your consciousness that is in opposition. When a negative thought comes into your mind, such as "How can you approve of yourself—you spent all of your money," or "You just ate two pieces of cake," or "You'll never amount to anything"—or whatever your negative babble may be, *this* is the time to take mental control. Give this thought no importance. Just see it for what it is—another way to keep you stuck in the past. Gently say to this thought, "Thank you for sharing. I let you go. I approve of myself." These thoughts of resistance will have no power over you unless you choose to believe them.

The statements listed in the checklist at the beginning of this chapter are listed again below, along with the affirmation corresponding to each belief. Make these affirmations part of your daily routine. Say them often in the car, at work, while looking in the mirror, or any time you feel your negative beliefs surfacing.

If You Believe:	Your Affirmation Could Be:
I want to relieve my pain *now*.	*I am at peace.*
Smoking cigarettes reduces my stress.	*I release my stress with deep breathing.*
Having lots of sex keeps me from thinking.	*I have the power, strength, and knowledge to handle everything in my life.*
I can't stop eating.	*I nourish myself with my own love.*
Drinking makes me popular.	*I radiate acceptance, and I am deeply loved by others.*
I need perfection.	*I release that silly belief. I am enough just as I am.*
I gamble too much.	*I am open to the wisdom within. I am at peace.*
I need my tranquilizers.	*I relax into the flow of life and let Life provide all that I need easily and comfortably.*
I can't stop buying things.	*I am willing to create new thoughts about myself and my life.*
I have a problem getting away from abusive relationships.	*No one can mistreat me. I love, appreciate, and respect myself.*

"I give myself permission to change."

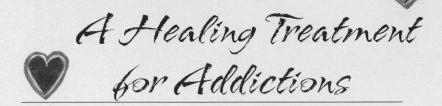

A Healing Treatment for Addictions

I am one with Life, and all of Life loves me

and supports me. Therefore, I claim for myself

high self-worth and self-esteem. I love and

appreciate myself on every level. I am not my

parents, nor any addictive pattern they may have

had. No matter what my past may have been,

now in this moment I choose to eliminate all

negative self-talk and to love and approve of

myself. I am my own unique self, and I rejoice

in who I am. I am acceptable and lovable. This

is the truth of my being, and I accept it as so.

All is well in my world.

Chapter Seven

FORGIVENESS

"I am forgiven, and I am free."

Forgiveness Checklist

☐ I'll never forgive them.

☐ What they did was unforgivable.

☐ They ruined my life.

☐ They did it on purpose.

☐ I was so little, and they hurt me so much.

☐ They have to apologize first.

☐ My resentment keeps me safe.

☐ Only weak people forgive.

☐ I'm right and they're wrong.

☐ It's all my parents' fault.

☐ I don't have to forgive anyone.

Do you resonate to several of these statements? Forgiveness is a difficult area for most of us.

We all need to do forgiveness work. Anyone who has a problem with loving themselves is stuck in this area. Forgiveness opens our hearts to self-love. Many of us carry grudges for years and years. We feel self-righteous because of what *they* did to us. I call this being stuck in the prison of self-righteous resentment. We get to be right. We never get to be happy.

I can hear you saying, "But you don't know what they did to me; it's unforgivable." Being unwilling to forgive is a terrible thing to do to ourselves. Bitterness is like swallowing a teaspoon of poison every day. It accumulates and harms us. It's impossible to be healthy and free when we keep ourselves bound to the past. The incident is long gone and over with. Yes, it's true that *they* didn't behave well. However, it's over. Sometimes we feel that if we forgive them, then we're saying that what they did to us was okay.

One of our biggest spiritual lessons is to understand that "everyone" is doing the best they can at any given moment. People can only do so much with the understanding, awareness, and knowledge that they have. Invariably, anyone who mistreats someone was mistreated themselves as a child. The greater the level of violence, the greater their own inner pain, and the more they may lash out. This is not to say that their behavior is acceptable or excusable. However, for our own spiritual growth, we must be aware of their pain.

The incident is over. Perhaps long over. Let it go. Allow yourself to be free. Come out of prison and step into the sunshine of life. If the incident is still going on, then ask yourself why you think so little of yourself that you still put up with it. Why do you stay in such a situation? The purpose of this book is to help you raise your self-esteem to such a level that you only allow loving experiences in your life. Don't waste time trying to "get even." It doesn't work. What we give out always comes back to us. So let's drop the past and work on loving ourselves in the *now*. Then we will have a wonderful future.

That person who is the hardest to forgive is the one who can teach you the greatest lessons. When you love yourself enough to rise above the old situation, then understanding and forgiveness will be easy. And you'll be free. Does freedom frighten you? Does it feel safer to be stuck in your old resentment and bitterness?

Mirror Work

It's time to go back to our friend, the mirror. Look into your eyes and say with feeling, "I am willing to forgive!" Repeat this several times.

What are you feeling? Do you feel stubborn and stuck, or do you feel open and willing?

Just notice your feelings. Don't judge them. Breathe deeply a few times, and repeat the process. Does it feel any different?

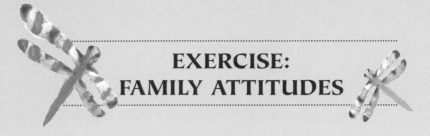

EXERCISE: FAMILY ATTITUDES

1. Was your mother a forgiving person?

_____

_____

_____

_____

_____

2. Was your father a forgiving person?

_____

_____

_____

_____

_____

3. Was bitterness a way of handling hurtful situations in your family?

_____

_____

_____

_____

_____

4. How did your mother get even?

_____

_____

_____

_____

_____

5. How did your father get even?

_____

_____

_____

_____

_____

6. How do you get even?

_____

_____

_____

_____

_____

7. Do you feel good when you get revenge?

_____

_____

_____

_____

8. Why do you feel this way?

_____

_____

_____

_____

An interesting phenomenon is that when we do our own forgiveness work, other people often respond to it. It's not necessary to go to the person involved and tell them that you forgive them. Sometimes you'll want to do this, but you don't have to. The major work in forgiveness is done in your own heart.

Forgiveness is seldom for "them." It's for us. The person you need to forgive may even be dead.

I've heard from many people who have truly forgiven someone, and then a month or two later, they may receive a phone call or a letter from the other person, asking to be forgiven. This seems to be particularly true when forgiveness exercises are done in front of a mirror, so as you do this exercise, notice how deep your feelings might be.

Mirror Work

Mirror work is often uncomfortable and something we may want to avoid. If you're standing in the bathroom doing mirror work, it's far too easy to run out the door. I believe that you receive the most benefits if you sit in front of a mirror. I like to use the big dressing mirror on the back of the bedroom door. I settle in with a box of tissues.

Give yourself time to do this exercise, or you can do it over and over. We all have lots of people to forgive.

Sit in front of your mirror. Close your eyes, and breathe deeply several times. Think of the many people who have hurt you in your life. Let them pass through your mind. Now open your eyes and begin talking to one of them.

Say something like: "You've hurt me deeply. However, I won't stay stuck in the past any longer. I am willing to forgive you." Take a breath and then say, "I forgive you, and I set you free." Breathe again and say, "You are free, and I am free."

Notice how you feel. You may feel resistance, or you may feel clear. If you feel resistance, just breathe and say, "I am willing to release all resistance."

This may be a day when you can forgive several people. It may be a day when you can forgive only one. It doesn't matter. No matter how you're doing this exercise, it's perfect for you. Forgiveness can be like peeling away the layers of an onion. If there are too many layers, put the onion away for a day. You can always come back and peel another layer. Acknowledge yourself for being willing to even begin this exercise.

As you continue to do this exercise, today or another day, expand your list of those to forgive. Remember:

- family members
- kids at school
- friends
- government agencies or figures
- medical professionals
- other authority figures
- teachers
- lovers
- co-workers
- church members or personnel
- God
- yourself

Most of all, forgive yourself. Stop being so hard on yourself. Self-punishment isn't necessary. You were doing the very best you could.

Sit in front of the mirror once again with your list. Say to each person on your list, "I forgive you for _____." Breathe. "I forgive you, and I set you free."

Continue to go down your list. If you feel that you're no longer angry or resentful toward someone, cross them off. If you're not free of anger, put them aside and come back to the work later.

As you continue to do this exercise, you'll find burdens melting off your shoulders. You may be surprised by the amount of old baggage you've been carrying. Be gentle with yourself as you go through the cleansing process.

EXERCISE: MAKE A LIST

Put on some soft music—something that will make you feel relaxed and peaceful. Now take a pad of paper and a pen and let your mind drift. Go back into the past, and think of all the things that you're angry with yourself about. Write them down. Write them *all* down. You may discover that you've never forgiven yourself for the humiliation of wetting your pants in the first grade. What a long time to carry *that* burden!

Sometimes it's easier to forgive others than to forgive ourselves. We're often hard on ourselves and demand perfection. Any mistakes we make are severely punished. It's time to go beyond that old attitude.

Mistakes are the way we learn. If we were perfect, there wouldn't be anything to learn. We wouldn't need to be on the planet. Being "perfect" will not get your parents' love and approval—it will only make you feel "wrong" and not good enough. Lighten up and stop treating yourself that way.

Forgive yourself. Let it go. Give yourself the space to be spontaneous and free. There's no need for shame and guilt.

Go outside to a beach, a park, or even a empty lot, and let yourself run. Don't jog. Run wild and free—turn somersaults, skip along the street—and laugh while you're doing it! Take your inner child with you and have some fun. So what if someone sees you? This is for your freedom!

The statements listed in the checklist at the beginning of this chapter are listed again below, along with the affirmation corresponding to each belief. Make these affirmations part of your daily routine. Say them often in the car, at work, while looking in the mirror, or any time you feel your negative beliefs surfacing.

If You Believe:

Your Affirmation Could Be:

If You Believe:	Your Affirmation Could Be:
I'll never forgive them.	This is a new moment. I am free to let go.
What they did was unforgivable.	I am willing to go beyond my own limitations.
They ruined my life.	I take responsibility for my own life. I am free.
They did it on purpose.	They were doing the best they could with the knowledge, understanding, and awareness that they had at the time.
I was so little, and they hurt me so much.	I am grown up now, and I take loving care of my inner child.
They have to apologize first.	My spiritual growth is not dependent on others.
My resentment keeps me safe.	I release myself from prison. I am safe and free.
Only weak people forgive.	It is empowering to forgive and let go.
I'm right, and they're wrong.	There is no right or wrong. I move beyond my judgment.
It's all my parents' fault.	My parents treated me in the way they *had* been treated. I forgive them—and their parents, too.
I don't have to forgive anyone.	I refuse to limit myself. I am always willing to take the next step.

"I give myself permission to let go."

Forgiveness Treatment

I am one with Life, and all of Life loves and
supports me. Therefore, I claim for myself an open
heart filled with love. We are all doing the best
we can at any given moment, and this is also true
for me. The past is over and done. I am not my
parents, nor their own patterns of resentment.
I am my own unique self, and I choose to open
my heart and allow the love, compassion, and
understanding to flush out all memories of past
pain. I am free to be all that I can be. This is
the truth of my being, and I accept it as so.
All is well in my life.

www.com

Chapter Eight

WORK

"It's a joy to express my creativity and be appreciated."

Work Checklist

☐ I hate my job.

☐ My job is too stressful.

☐ No one appreciates me at work.

☐ I always get dead-end jobs.

☐ My boss is abusive.

☐ Everyone expects too much of me.

☐ My co-workers drive me crazy.

☐ My job offers no creativity.

☐ I'll never be successful.

☐ There's no chance for advancement.

☐ My job doesn't pay well.

Let's explore your thinking in the work area. Our jobs and the work that we do are a reflection of our own self-worth and our value to the world. On one level, work is an exchange of time and services for money. I like to believe that all forms of business are opportunities for us to bless and prosper each other.

The *kind* of work we do is important to us because we're unique individuals. We want to feel that we're making a contribution to the world. We need to express our own talents, intelligence, and creative ability.

There are problems that can occur in the workplace, though. You may not get along with your boss or your co-workers. You may not feel appreciated or recognized for the work that you do. Promotional opportunities or a specific job may elude you.

Remember that whatever position you may find yourself in . . . your thinking got you there. The people around you are only mirroring what *you* believe you deserve.

Thoughts can be changed, and situations can be changed as well. That boss whom we find intolerable could become our champion. That dead-end position with no hope of advancement may open up a new career full of possibilities. The co-worker who is so annoying might turn out to be, if not a friend, at least someone who's easier to get along with. The salary that we find insufficient can increase in the twinkle of an eye. We could find a wonderful new job.

There are an infinite number of channels if we can change our thinking. Let's open ourselves up to all the possibilities. We must accept in consciousness that abundance and fulfillment can come from anywhere. The change may be small at first, such as an additional assignment from your boss in which you could demonstrate your intelligence and creativity. You might find that if you don't treat a co-worker like they're the enemy, a noticeable change in behavior may occur. Whatever the change may be, accept and rejoice in it. You're not alone. You *are* the change. The Power that created you has given *you* the power to create your own experiences!

EXERCISE: CENTER YOURSELF

Let's take a moment to center ourselves. Take your right hand and place it over your lower stomach area. Think of this area as the center of your being. Breathe. Look into your mirror again, and say, *"I am willing to release the need to be so unhappy at work."* Say it two more times. Each time, say it in a different way. What you want to do is increase your commitment to change.

EXERCISE: DESCRIBE THE PEOPLE IN YOUR WORK ENVIRONMENT

Use ten adjectives to describe your:

	Boss	Co-workers	Position
1.			
2.			
3.			
4.			
5.			
6.			
7.			
8.			
9.			
10.			

EXERCISE: THINK ABOUT
YOUR WORK LIFE

1. If you could become anything, what would you be?

_____

_____

_____

_____

_____

_____

2. If you could have any job that you wanted, what would
   it be?

_____

_____

_____

_____

_____

_____

3. What would you like to change about your current job?

4. What would you change about your employer?

5. Do you work in a pleasant environment?

_____

_____

_____

_____

_____

6. Whom do you need to forgive the most at work?

_____

_____

_____

_____

_____

Mirror Work

Sit in front of your mirror. Breathe deeply. Center yourself. Now talk to the person at work you're the most angry with. Tell them why you're angry. Tell them how much they've hurt you, threatened you, or violated your space and boundaries. Tell them everything—don't hold back! Tell them about the kind of behavior you want from them in the future. Tell them that you forgive them for not being who you wanted them to be.

Take a breath. Ask them to give you respect, and offer the same to them. Affirm that you can both have a harmonious working relationship.

Blessing with Love

Blessing with love is a powerful tool to use in any work environment. Send it ahead of you before you arrive at your place of employment. Bless every person, place, or thing there with love. If you have a problem with a co-worker, a boss, a supplier, or even the temperature in the building, bless it with love. Affirm that you and the person or situation are in agreement and in perfect harmony:

"I am in perfect harmony with my work environment and everyone in it."

"I always work in harmonious surroundings."

"I honor and respect each person, and they, in turn, honor and respect me."

"I bless this situation with love and know that it works out the best for everyone concerned."

"I bless you with love and release you to your highest good."

"I bless this job and release it to someone who will love it, and I am free to accept a wonderful new opportunity."

Select or adapt one of these affirmations to fit a situation in your workplace, and repeat it over and over. Every time the person or situation comes to mind, repeat the affirmation. Eliminate the negative energy in your mind regarding this situation. You can, just by thinking, change the experience.

EXERCISE: SELF-WORTH IN YOUR JOB

Let's examine your feelings of self-worth in the area of employment. After answering the following questions, write an affirmation (in the present tense).

1. **Do I feel worthy of having a good job?**

    Sample Answer: *Sometimes I don't feel good enough.*

    Sample Affirmation: *I am totally adequate for all situations.*

    Your Answer:

    _____

    _____

Your Affirmation:

_____

_____

2. **What do I fear most about work?**

Sample Answer: *My employer will find out that I'm no good, will fire me, and I won't find another job.*

Sample Affirmation: *I center myself in safety and accept the perfection of my life. All is well.*

Your Answer:

_____

_____

Your Affirmation:

_____

_____

3. **What am I "getting" from this belief?**

Sample Answer: *I people-please at work, and turn my employer into a parent.*

Sample Affirmation: *It's my mind that creates my experiences. I am unlimited in my ability to create the good in my life.*

Your Answer:

_____

_____

Your Affirmation:

_____

_____

4. **What do I fear will happen if I let go of this belief?**

    Sample Answer: _I would have to grow up and be responsible._

    Sample Affirmation: _I know that I am worthwhile. It is safe for me to succeed. Life loves me._

    Your Answer:

    _____

    _____

    Your Affirmation:

    _____

    _____

Visualization

What would the perfect job be? Take a moment to see yourself in the job. Visualize yourself in the environment, see your co-workers, and feel what it would be like to do work that's completely fulfilling—while you earn a good salary. Hold that vision for yourself, and know that it has been fulfilled in consciousness.

The statements listed in the checklist at the beginning of this chapter are listed again below, along with the affirmation corresponding to each belief. Make these affirmations part of your daily routine. Say them often in the car, at work, while looking in the mirror, or any time you feel your negative beliefs surfacing.

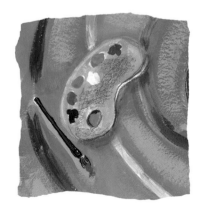

If You Believe:	Your Affirmation Could Be:
I hate my job.	*I enjoy the work I do and the people I work with.*
My job is too stressful.	*I am always relaxed at work.*
No one appreciates me at work.	*My work is recognized by everyone.*
I always get dead-end jobs.	*I turn every experience into an opportunity.*
My boss is abusive.	*All my bosses treat me with love and respect.*
Everyone expects too much of me.	*I am capable and competent and in the perfect place.*
My co-workers drive me crazy.	*I see the best in everyone, and they respond in kind.*
My job offers no creativity.	*My thoughts create a wonderful new opportunity.*
I'll never be successful.	*Everything I touch from now on is a success.*
There's no chance for advancement.	*New doors are opening all the time.*
My job doesn't pay well.	*I am open and receptive to new avenues of income.*

"I give myself permission to be creatively fulfilled."

Work Treatment

I am one with Life, and all of Life loves and supports me. Therefore, I claim for myself the best creative self-expression possible. My work environment is deeply fulfilling to me. I am loved, appreciated, and respected at work. I am not my parents, nor their own patterns of work experience. I am my own unique self, and I choose to do work that brings me even more satisfaction than the money. Work has become a joy for me. This is the truth of my being, and I accept it as so. All is well in my working world.

Chapter Nine

MONEY AND PROSPERITY

"Infinite prosperity is mine to share; I am blessed."

Money and Prosperity Checklist

- [ ] I can't save money.
- [ ] I don't earn enough.
- [ ] My credit rating is bad.
- [ ] Money slips through my fingers.
- [ ] Everything is so expensive.
- [ ] Why does everyone else have money?
- [ ] I can't pay my bills.
- [ ] Bankruptcy is around the corner.
- [ ] I can't save for retirement.
- [ ] I can't let go of money.

What are your beliefs about money? Do you believe that there's enough? Do you attach your self-worth to it? Do you think that it will bring you your heart's desire? Are you friends with money, or is it an enemy?

Having more money is not enough. We need to learn how to *deserve* and *enjoy* the money we have.

Large amounts of money do not guarantee prosperity. People who have a lot of money can be engulfed in poverty consciousness. They can be more fearful about not having money than a homeless person who lives on the street. The ability to enjoy their money and to live in a world of abundance may elude them. Socrates, the great philosopher, once said that "contentment is natural wealth; luxury is artificial poverty."

As I've said many times, your prosperity consciousness is not dependent upon money; your flow of money is dependent upon your prosperity consciousness.

Our pursuit of money *must* contribute to the quality of our lives. If it doesn't—that is, if we hate what we do in order to make money, then money will be useless. Prosperity involves the *quality* of our lives, as well as any amount of money that we possess.

Prosperity is not defined by money alone; it encompasses time, love, success, joy, comfort, beauty, and wisdom. For example, you can be poor with respect to time. If you feel rushed, pressured, and harried, then your time is steeped in poverty. But if you feel you have all the time you need to finish any task at hand, and you're confident that you can finish any job, then you're prosperous when it comes to time.

Or what about success? Do you feel that it's beyond your

reach and completely unattainable? Or do you feel that you can be a success in your own right? If you do, then you're rich with respect to success.

Know that whatever your beliefs are, they can be changed in *this* moment. The power that created you has given *you* the power to create your own experiences. You can change!

Mirror Work

Stand up with your arms outstretched, and say, *"I am open and receptive to all good."* How does that feel?

Now, look into the mirror and say it again with feeling.

What kinds of feelings come up for you? Does it feel liberating to _____ (you fill in the blank). Do this exercise every morning. It's a wonderfully symbolic gesture that may increase your prosperity consciousness and bring more good into your life.

EXERCISE: YOUR FEELINGS ABOUT MONEY

Let's examine your feelings of self-worth in this area. Answer the following questions as best you can.

1. Go back to the mirror. Look into your eyes and say, "My biggest fear about money is _____."
    Write down your answer and tell why you feel that way.

    _____

    _____

    _____

    _____

    _____

2. What did you learn about money as a child?

    _____

    _____

    _____

    _____

3. Did your parents grow up during the Depression era?
    What were their thoughts about money?

    _____

    _____

    _____

    _____

    _____

4. How were finances handled in your family?

    _____

    _____

    _____

    _____

    _____

    _____

5.   How do you handle money now?

_____

_____

_____

_____

_____

6.   What would you like to change about your money
      consciousness?

_____

_____

_____

_____

_____

EXERCISE: YOUR MONEY CONSCIOUSNESS

Let's further examine your feelings of self-worth in the money area. Answer the following questions as best you can. After each negative belief, create a positive affirmation in the present tense to take its place.

1. **Do I feel worthy of having and enjoying money?**

   Sample Answer: *Not really. I get rid of money as soon as I get it.*

   Sample Affirmation: *I bless the money I have. It is safe to save money and let my money work for me.*

   Your Answer:

   _____

   _____

   Your Affirmation:

   _____

   _____

2. **What is my greatest fear regarding money?**

    Sample Answer: *I'm afraid that I'll always be broke.*

    Sample Affirmation: *I now accept limitless abundance from a limitless Universe.*

    Your Answer:

    _____

    _____

    Your Affirmation:

    _____

    _____

3. **What am I "getting" from this belief?**

    Sample Answer: *I get to stay poor, and I get to be taken care of by others.*

    Sample Affirmation: *I claim my own power and lovingly create my own reality. I trust the process of life.*

    Your Answer:

    _____

    _____

Your Affirmation:

_____

_____

4. **What do I fear will happen to me if I let go of this belief?**

    Sample Answer: *No one will love me and take care of me.*

    Sample Affirmation: *I am safe in the Universe, and all life loves and supports me.*

    Your Answer:

    _____

    _____

    Your Affirmation:

    _____

    _____

EXERCISE: YOUR USE OF MONEY

Write down three ways in which you're critical of your use of money. Maybe you're constantly in debt, you can't save money, or you can't enjoy your money.

Think of one example in each of these instances where you *haven't* acted out the undesirable behavior.

Examples:

I criticize myself for: *compulsively spending money and being in constant debt. I can't seem to hold down my spending.*

I praise myself for: *paying the rent today. It's the first of the month, and I am making my payment on time.*

I criticize myself for: *saving every penny that I make. I can't let go of my money.*

I praise myself for: *buying a shirt that wasn't on sale. I let myself have what I really wanted today.*

1. **I criticize myself for:**

_____

_____

_____

_____

I praise myself for:

_____

_____

_____

_____

2. **I criticize myself for:**

_____

_____

_____

_____

_____

I praise myself for:

_____

_____

_____

_____

3.   I criticize myself for:

_____

_____

_____

_____

_____

_____

I praise myself for:

_____

_____

_____

_____

_____

_____

Visualizations

Place your hand over your heart, take a few deep breaths, and relax. See yourself acting out your worst scenario with money. Perhaps you borrowed money that you couldn't return, bought something you knew you couldn't afford, or declared bankruptcy. See yourself acting out the behavior—*love that person that you were*. Know that you were doing the very best you could with the knowledge, understanding, and capability that you had. *Love that person*. See yourself acting out behavior that might embarrass you today, and *love that person*.

What would it be like to have all of the things you've always wanted? What would they look like? Where would you go? What would you do? Feel it. Enjoy it. Be creative and *have fun*.

The statements listed in the checklist at the beginning of this chapter are listed again below, along with the affirmation corresponding to each belief. Make these affirmations part of your daily routine. Say them often in the car, at work, while looking in the mirror, or any time you feel your negative beliefs surfacing.

If You Believe:	*Your Affirmation Could Be:*
I can't save money.	*I am worthy of having money in the bank.*
I don't earn enough.	*My income is constantly increasing.*
My credit rating is bad.	*My credit rating is getting better all the time.*
Money slips through my fingers.	*I spend money wisely.*
Everything is so expensive.	*I always have as much as I need.*
Why does everyone else have money?	*I have as much money as I can accept.*
I can't pay my bills.	*I bless all of my bills with love. I pay them on time.*
Bankruptcy is around the corner.	*I will always be financially solvent.*
I can't save for retirement.	*I am joyfully providing for my retirement.*
I can't let go of money.	*I enjoy saving, and I spend in balance.*

"I give myself permission to prosper."

Money and
Prosperity Treatment

I am one with Life, and all of Life loves and supports me. Therefore, I claim for myself an abundant share of the prosperity of life. I have an abundance of time, love, joy, comfort, beauty, wisdom, success, and money. I am not my parents, nor their own financial patterns. I am my own unique self, and I choose to be open and receptive to prosperity in all its many forms. I am deeply grateful to Life for all its generosity to me. My income constantly increases, and I continue to prosper for the rest of my life. This is the truth of my being, and I accept it as so. All is well in my prosperous world.

Chapter Ten

FRIENDS

"I am a friend to myself."

Friendship Checklist

☐ My friends don't support me.

☐ Everyone is so judgmental.

☐ Nobody sees it my way.

☐ My boundaries are not respected.

☐ I can't keep friends for too long.

☐ I can't let my friends really know me.

☐ I give my friends advice for their own good.

☐ I don't know how to be a friend.

☐ I don't know how to ask for help from my friends.

☐ I don't know how to say no to a friend.

Friendships can be our most enduring and important relationships. We can live without lovers or spouses. We can live without our primary families. But most of us cannot live happily without friends. I believe that we choose our parents before we're born into this planet, but we choose our friends on a more conscious level.

Ralph Waldo Emerson, the great American philosopher and writer, wrote an essay on friendship, calling it the "nectar of the gods." He explained that in romantic relationships, one person is always trying to change the other, but friends can stand back and look at one another with appreciation and respect.

Friends can be an extension or a substitute for the nuclear family. There's a great need in most of us to share life experiences with others. Not only do we learn more about others when we engage in friendship, but we can also learn more about ourselves. These relationships are mirrors of our self-worth and esteem. They afford us the perfect opportunity to look at ourselves, and the areas where we might need to grow.

When the bond between friends becomes strained, we can look to the negative messages of childhood. It may be time for mental housecleaning. Cleaning the mental house after a lifetime of negative messages is a bit like starting a sound nutritional program after a lifetime of eating junk foods. As you change your diet, your body will throw off a toxic residue, and you may feel worse for a day or two.

So it is when you make a decision to change your mental thought patterns. Your circumstances may worsen for a while, but remember—you may have to dig through a lot of dry weed to get to the rich soil below. But you can do it! I know you can!

EXERCISE:
YOUR FRIENDSHIPS

In the space provided below, write the following affirmation three times:

"I am willing to release any pattern in me that creates troubled friendships."

_____

_____

_____

_____

_____

_____

1. What were your first childhood friendships like?

_____

_____

_____

_____

_____

_____

2. How are your friendships today like those childhood friendships?

_____

_____

_____

_____

_____

_____

3. What did you learn about friendship from your parents?

_____

_____

_____

_____

_____

4. What kind of friends did your parents have?

_____

_____

_____

_____

_____

5. What kind of friends would you like to have in the future? Be specific.

   _____

   _____

   _____

   _____

   _____

EXERCISE: SELF-WORTH AND FRIENDSHIP

Let's examine your self-worth in the area of friendship. Answer each of the following questions below. After each question, write a positive affirmation (in the present tense) to replace the old belief.

1. **Do I feel worthy of having good friends?**

   Sample Answer: *No. Why would anyone want to be around me?*

   Sample Affirmation: *I love and accept myself, and I am a magnet for friends.*

Your Answer:

_____

_____

Your Affirmation:

_____

_____

2. **What do I fear most about having close friends?**

Sample Answer: *I am afraid of betrayal. I don't feel that I can trust anyone.*

Sample Affirmation: *I trust myself, I trust life, and I trust my friends.*

Your Answer:

_____

_____

Your Affirmation:

_____

_____

3. **What am I "getting" from this belief?**

Sample Answer: *I get to be judgmental. I wait for my friends to make one false move so that I can make them wrong.*

Sample Affirmation: *All of my friendships are successful. I am a loving and nurturing friend.*

Your Answer:

_____

_____

Your Affirmation:

_____

_____

4. **What do I fear will happen if I let go of this belief?**

Sample Answer: *I'll lose control. I'd have to let people really get to know me.*

Sample Affirmation: *Loving others is easy when I love and accept myself.*

Your Answer:

_____

_____

Your Affirmation:

_____

_____

If we're all responsible for the events in our lives, then there's no one to blame. Whatever is happening "out there" is only a reflection of our own inner thinking.

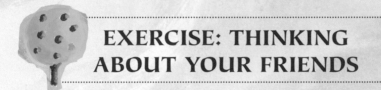 ## EXERCISE: THINKING ABOUT YOUR FRIENDS

Think of three events in your life where you feel you were mistreated or abused by friends. Perhaps a friend betrayed a confidence or abandoned you in a time of need. Maybe this person interfered with a spouse or mate.

In each case, name the event, and write down the thoughts you had at the time that preceded each event.

Sample Event: *When I was 16 years old, my best friend Susie turned on me and started to spread vicious rumors. When I tried to confront her, she lied to me. I was friendless my entire senior year.*

Sample Thoughts: *I did not deserve friends. I was drawn to my friend Susie because she was cold and judgmental. I was used to being judged and criticized.*

1. **The Event:**

_____

_____

_____

_____

My Deepest Thoughts Were:

_____

_____

_____

_____

2. **The Event:**

_____

_____

_____

_____

My Deepest Thoughts Were:

_____

_____

_____

_____

3. **The Event:**

_____

_____

_____

_____

My Deepest Thoughts Were:

_____

_____

_____

_____

EXERCISE: THE SUPPORT OF YOUR FRIENDS

Think of three events in your life where you were supported by friends. Perhaps a good friend stood up for you or gave you money when you needed it. Maybe this person helped you resolve a difficult situation.

In each case, name the event, and write down the thoughts you had at the time that preceded each event.

Sample Event: *I'll always remember Helen. When people at my first job were making fun of me because I said something stupid at a meeting, Helen stood up for me. She helped me through my embarrassment and saved my job.*

My Deepest Thoughts Were: *Even if I make a mistake, someone will always help me. I deserve to be supported. Women support me.*

1.   **The Event:**

   _____

   _____

   _____

   _____

My Deepest Thoughts Were:

_____

_____

_____

_____

_____

2. The Event:

_____

_____

_____

_____

_____

My Deepest Thoughts Were:

_____

_____

_____

_____

3.   The Event:

_____

_____

_____

_____

_____

My Deepest Thoughts Were:

_____

_____

_____

_____

Visualizations

Which friends do you need to acknowledge? Take a moment to visualize them. Look those people in the eye and say: *"I thank you and bless you with love for being there for me when I needed you. May your life be filled with joy."*

Which friends do you need to forgive? Take a moment to visualize them. Look at those people in the eye and say: *"I forgive you for not acting the way I wanted you to. I forgive you and I set you free."*

The statements listed in the checklist at the beginning of this chapter are listed again below, along with the affirmation corresponding to each belief. Make these affirmations part of your daily routine. Say them often in the car, at work, while looking in the mirror, or any time you feel your negative beliefs surfacing.

If You Believe:	Your Affirmation Could Be:
My friends don't support me.	My friends are loving and supportive.
Everyone is so judgmental.	As I release all criticism, judgmental people leave my life.
Nobody sees it my way.	I am open and receptive to all points of view.
My boundaries are not respected.	I respect others, and they respect me.
I can't keep friends for too long.	My love and acceptance of others creates lasting friendships.
I can't let my friends really know me.	It's safe for me to be open.
I give my friends advice for their own good.	I leave my friends alone. We both have total freedom to be ourselves.
I don't know how to be a friend.	I trust my inner wisdom to guide me.
I don't know how to ask for help from my friends.	It's safe for me to ask for what I want.
I don't know how to say no to a friend.	I move beyond those limitations and express myself honestly.

"I give myself permission to be a friend."

Friendship Treatment

I am one with Life, and all of Life loves and

supports me. Therefore, I claim for myself a

joyous, loving circle of friends. We all have

such good times individually and together. I am

not my parents nor their relationships. I am my

own unique self, and I choose to only allow

supportive, nurturing people in my world.

Wherever I go I am greeted with warmth and

friendliness. I deserve the best friends, and I allow

my life to be filled with love and joy. This is the

truth of my being, and I accept it as so. All is

well in my friendly world.

Chapter Eleven

SEXUALITY

"I am at peace with my own sexuality."

Sexuality Checklist

- ☐ I'm afraid of sex.
- ☐ Sex is dirty.
- ☐ Genitals frighten me.
- ☐ I'm too fat/thin to be sexy
- ☐ I'm ashamed of my sexuality.
- ☐ I can't ask for what I want.
- ☐ God doesn't want me to be sexual.
- ☐ I'm afraid that my partner won't like my body.
- ☐ I'm afraid of dis-ease.
- ☐ I'm not good enough.
- ☐ Sex is painful.

Sex is a difficult area for a lot of people. Many complain that they're getting too much or too little. Sex threatens them, motivates them, maddens them, and offers escape. It can be tender, loving, joyful, painful, explosive, wondrous, fulfilling, or humiliating.

People often equate sex with love, or they need to be in love to have sex. Many of us grew up believing that sex was sinful unless we were married, or that sex was for procreation and not for pleasure. Some people have rebelled against this concept and feel that sex has nothing to do with love.

Most of our beliefs about sex can be traced to our childhood and our ideas about God and religion. Most of us were raised with the idea of what I call "Mama's God," which is what your mother taught you about God when you were very little. It's often the image of God as an old man with a beard. This old man sits on a cloud and stares at people's genitals, waiting to catch someone sinning.

Think for a moment about the vastness of the Universe. How perfect it all is! Think about the level of intelligence that created it. I have a difficult time believing that this same Divine intelligence could resemble a judgmental old man watching *my* genitals.

When we were babies, we knew how perfect our bodies were, and we loved our sexuality. Babies are never ashamed of themselves. *No baby measures its hips to find its self-worth.*

We must let go of images and beliefs that do not nourish and support us. I believe that the sexual revolution, which occurred in the late 1960s, was a good thing in many ways. We were freed from Victorian ideas and hypocrisy. Of course, when people are freed from oppression, they go wild for a while. Eventually, the pendulum will swing back until it reaches a balance point—neither too wild nor too oppressed. I believe that sex is meant to be a joyful, loving act, and as long as our hearts are open and we really care about ourselves, we won't harm ourselves or others. However, sex can be another form of abuse, and an expression of low self-esteem. If we constantly need a new partner to make us feel worthy, or if we allow infidelity to be a way of life, we need to examine our thinking.

Visualization

Before you answer the following questions, lie down or sit in a comfortable position. Close your eyes, and put both hands over your heart. Picture a stream of brilliant white light entering your heart. Focus on the vision of light, and say out loud: "I am willing to let the love in." Feel the energy flowing into your heart. After a few minutes, repeat this several times, open your eyes, and say: "All is well."

189

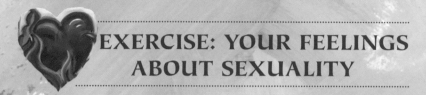

EXERCISE: YOUR FEELINGS ABOUT SEXUALITY

Answer the following questions as best you can.

1. What did you learn about sex as a child?

    _____

    _____

    _____

    _____

    _____

2. What did your parents teach you about the human body? Was it beautiful, or was it something to be ashamed of?

    _____

    _____

    _____

    _____

    _____

3. What did your teachers or your church say about sex?
    Was it a sin to be punished for?

    _____

    _____

    _____

    _____

    _____

4. What were your genitals called? Or were they just
    something "down there"?

    _____

    _____

    _____

    _____

    _____

5. Do you think that your parents had a fulfilling sex life?

_____

_____

_____

_____

_____

6. How are your ideas about sex similar to those your parents taught you?

_____

_____

_____

_____

_____

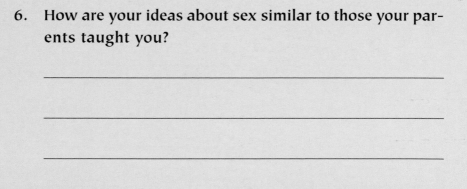

7. How are they different?

_____

_____

_____

_____

_____

8. What did God "think" about sex when you were little?

_____

_____

_____

_____

_____

9. Do you equate sex with love?

    _____

    _____

    _____

    _____

    _____

    _____

10. How do you feel during the sex act itself? Do you feel
    loving and tender? Do you feel powerful? Do you feel
    guilty?

    _____

    _____

    _____

    _____

    _____

11. Have you ever abused yourself or another sexually?

_____

_____

_____

_____

_____

_____

12. Have you ever been abused sexually?

_____

_____

_____

_____

_____

_____

13. If you could change anything about sex in your life, what would it be?

_____

_____

_____

_____

_____

Mirror Work

Now look into your own eyes in the mirror, and say: *"I am willing to love my body and my sexuality."* Say it three times with more meaning and feeling each time. Then, answer these questions.

I. What are your most negative thoughts about your body?

_____

_____

_____

_____

2. Where did these thoughts come from?

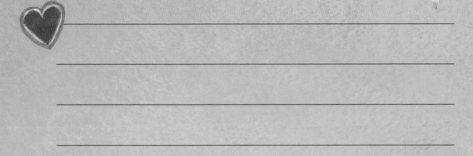

_____

_____

_____

_____

_____

3. Are you willing to release them? Yes? No? Not yet?

_____

_____

_____

_____

_____

Now let's examine the issue of self-worth. Answer these questions, and after each one, create a corresponding affirmation.

1. **Do I deserve to enjoy my sexuality?**

    Sample Answer: *No. I hate the shape of my body. I want to hurry up and get sex over with. I feel ugly.*

    Sample Affirmation: *I love and appreciate my beautiful body. It's the perfect size and shape for me. I rejoice in my sexuality.*

    Your Answer:

    _____

    _____

    Your Affirmation:

    _____

    _____

2. **What do I fear most about my sexuality?**

    Sample Answer: *I fear being laughed at. I'm afraid of doing it wrong or not knowing what to do. I'm afraid of feeling dirty.*

    Sample Affirmation: *My sexuality is a wonderful gift. I love being creative. I am safe.*

Your Answer:

_____

_____

Your Affirmation:

_____

_____

3. **What am I "getting" from this belief?**

    Sample Answer: *I get protection. I get to feel safe. I don't want anyone coming close to me with their genitals. Genitals scare me.*

    Sample Affirmation: *It's safe to be myself. I love all of my body. I trust in the life process to keep me safe.*

    Your Answer:

    _____

    _____

    Your Affirmation:

    _____

    _____

4. **What do I fear will happen if I let go of this belief?**

Sample Answer: *I'll lose control. I'm afraid that I'll get lost. There will be no more "me."*

Sample Affirmation: *I am safe to be me in all situations. I rejoice in my individuality.*

Your Answer:

_____

_____

Your Affirmation:

_____

_____

The statements listed in the checklist at the beginning of this chapter are listed again below, along with the affirmation corresponding to each belief. Make these affirmations part of your daily routine. Say them often in the car, at work, while looking in the mirror, or any time you feel your negative beliefs surfacing.

If You Believe:	Your Affirmation Could Be:
I'm afraid of sex.	It is safe for me to explore my sexuality.
Sex is dirty.	Sex is tender, loving, and joyful.
Genitals frighten me.	Genitals are normal, natural, and beautiful.
I'm too fat/thin to be sexual.	I am a sexual being no matter what size I am.
I'm ashamed of my sexuality.	I go beyond limiting beliefs and accept myself totally.
I can't ask for what I want.	I express my desires with joy and freedom.
God doesn't want me to be sexual.	God created and approves of my sexuality.
I'm afraid that my partner won't like my body.	My partner reflects the love I have for my own body.
I'm afraid of dis-ease.	I respect myself, and I am divinely protected and guided.
I'm not good enough.	I love myself and my sexuality. I am at peace.
Sex is painful.	I am gentle with my body, and so is my partner.

"I give myself permission to enjoy my body."

Sexuality Treatment

I am one with Life, and all of Life loves and supports me. Therefore, I claim for myself complete acceptance of my sexuality and its expression. I love my body and its sexuality. I am not my parents, nor their sexual patterns. I am my own unique self, and I choose to love every part of my body and all its functions. My liver, my nose, my toes, and my genitals are all wondrously made and lovable. I only share my body with those who deeply love and respect me. I rejoice in my sexuality. This is the truth of my being, and I accept it as so. All is well with my sexuality.

Chapter Twelve

LOVE AND INTIMACY

"Love surrounds me. I am loving, lovable, and loved."

Love and Intimacy Checklist

- [ ] I'm afraid of rejection.
- [ ] Love never lasts.
- [ ] I feel trapped.
- [ ] Love scares me.
- [ ] I have to do everything *their* way.
- [ ] If I take care of myself, they'll leave me.
- [ ] I'm jealous.
- [ ] I can't be myself.
- [ ] I'm not good enough.
- [ ] I don't want a marriage like my parents had.
- [ ] I don't know how to love.
- [ ] I'll get hurt.
- [ ] I can't say no to someone I love.
- [ ] Everybody leaves me.

How did you experience love as a child? Did you observe your parents expressing love and affection? Were you raised with lots of hugs? Or in your family, was love expressed through fighting, yelling, crying, door-slamming, manipulation, control, silence, or revenge? If it was, then you'll most likely seek out similar experiences as an adult. You'll find people who will reinforce those ideas. If, as a child, you looked for love and found pain, then as an adult, you'll find pain instead of love . . . unless you release your old family patterns.

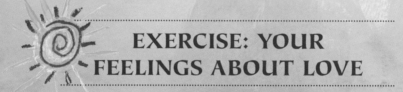

EXERCISE: YOUR FEELINGS ABOUT LOVE

Answer the following questions as best you can.

1.   How did your last relationship end?

_____

_____

_____

_____

_____

2. How did the one before that end?

_____

_____

_____

_____

_____

3. Think about your last two intimate relationships. What were the major issues between you?

_____

_____

_____

_____

_____

4. **How did these issues remind you of your relationship with one or both or your parents?**

_____

_____

_____

_____

_____

_____

Perhaps all of your relationships ended as a result of your partner leaving you. The need in you to be left could stem from a family divorce, a parent withdrawing from you because you weren't what they wanted you to be, or a death in the family.

To change the pattern, you need to forgive your parent *and* understand that you don't have to repeat this old behavior. You free them, and you free yourself.

For every habit or pattern we repeat over and over again, there's a *need within us* for such repetition. The need corresponds to some belief that we have. If there was no need, we would not have to have it, do it, or be it. Self-criticism does not break the pattern—letting go of the need does.

Mirror Work

Using your mirror, look into your eyes, breathe, and say: *"I am willing to release the need for relationships that don't nourish and support me."* Say this five times in the mirror; each time you say it, give it more meaning. Think of some of your relationships as you say it.

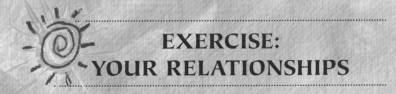

EXERCISE: YOUR RELATIONSHIPS

In the space below, answer the following questions as best you can.

1. **What did you learn about love as a child?**

_____

_____

_____

_____

_____

_____

2. Did you ever have a boss who was "just like" one of your parents? How?

_____

_____

_____

_____

_____

3. Is your partner/spouse like one of your parents? How?

_____

_____

_____

_____

_____

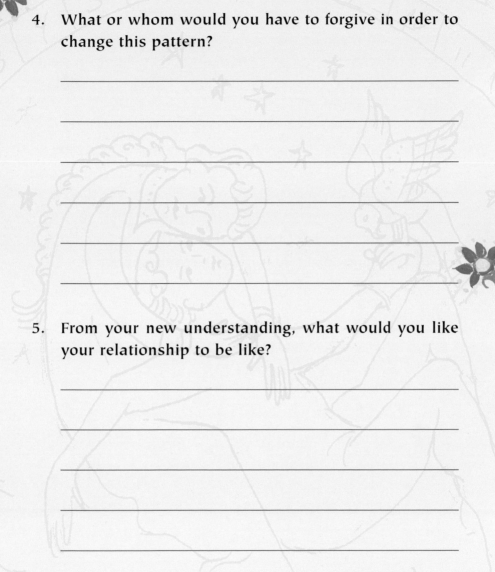

4. What or whom would you have to forgive in order to
    change this pattern?

    _____

    _____

    _____

    _____

    _____

5. From your new understanding, what would you like
    your relationship to be like?

    _____

    _____

    _____

    _____

    _____

Your old thoughts and beliefs continue to form your experiences until you let them go. Your future thoughts haven't been formed, and you don't know what they'll be. Your current thought, the one you're thinking right now, is totally under your control.

We are the only ones who choose our thoughts. We may habitually think the same thought over and over so that it doesn't seem as if we're choosing the thought. But we did make the original choice. However, we *can* refuse to think certain thoughts. How often have you refused to think a *positive* thought about yourself? Well, you can also refuse to think a *negative* thought about yourself. It just takes practice.

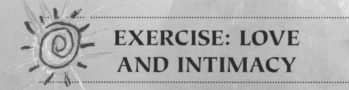

EXERCISE: LOVE AND INTIMACY

Let's examine these beliefs. Answer each of the questions below. After each answer, write a positive affirmation (in the present tense) to replace the old belief.

1.   **Do I feel worthy of having an intimate relationship?**

Sample Answer: *No. Another person would run if they really knew me.*

Sample Affirmation: *I am lovable and worth knowing.*

Your Answer:

_____

_____

Your Affirmation:

_____

_____

2. Am I afraid to love?

    Sample Answer: *Yes. I'm afraid that my mate won't be faithful.*

    Sample Affirmation: *I am always secure in love.*

    Your Answer:

    _____

    _____

    Your Affirmation:

    _____

    _____

3. **What am I "getting" from this belief?**

Sample Answer: *I don't let romance into my life.*

Sample Affirmation: *It is safe for me to open my heart to let love in.*

Your Answer:

_____

_____

Your Affirmation:

_____

_____

4. **What do I fear will happen if I let go of this belief?**

Sample Answer: *I'll be taken advantage of and be hurt.*

Sample Affirmation: *It is safe for me to share my inner-most self with others.*

Your Answer:

_____

_____

Your Affirmation:

_____

_____

The statements listed in the checklist at the beginning of this chapter are listed again below, along with the affirmation corresponding to each belief. Make these affirmations part of your daily routine. Say them often in the car, at work, while looking in the mirror, or any time you feel your negative beliefs surfacing.

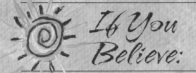

If You Believe:	Your Affirmation Could Be:
I'm afraid of rejection.	I love and accept myself, and I am safe.
Love never lasts.	Love is eternal.
I feel trapped.	Love makes me feel free.
Love scares me.	It is safe for me to be in love.
I have to do everything *their* way.	We are always equal partners.
If I take care of myself, they'll leave me.	We each take care of ourselves.
I'm jealous.	Jealousy is only insecurity. I now develop my own self-esteem.
I can't be myself.	People love me when I am myself.
I'm not good enough.	I am worthy of love.
I don't want a marriage like my parents had.	I am not my parents. I go beyond their patterns.
I don't know how to love.	Loving myself and others gets easier every day.
I'll get hurt.	The more I open up to love, the safer I am.
I can't say no to someone I love.	My partner and I respect each other's decisions.
Everybody leaves me.	I now create a long-lasting, loving relationship.

"I give myself permission to experience intimate love."

Love and Intimacy Treatment

I am one with Life, and all of Life loves and
supports me. Therefore, I claim love and intimacy
in my world. I am worthy of love. I am not my
parents, nor their own relationship patterns.
I am my own unique self, and I choose to create
and keep a long-lasting, loving relationship—
one that nurtures and supports us both in every
way. We have great compatibility and similar
rhythms, and we bring out the best in each other.
We're romantic, and we're the best of friends.
I rejoice in this long-term relationship. This is
the truth of my being, and I accept it as so.
All is well in my loving world.

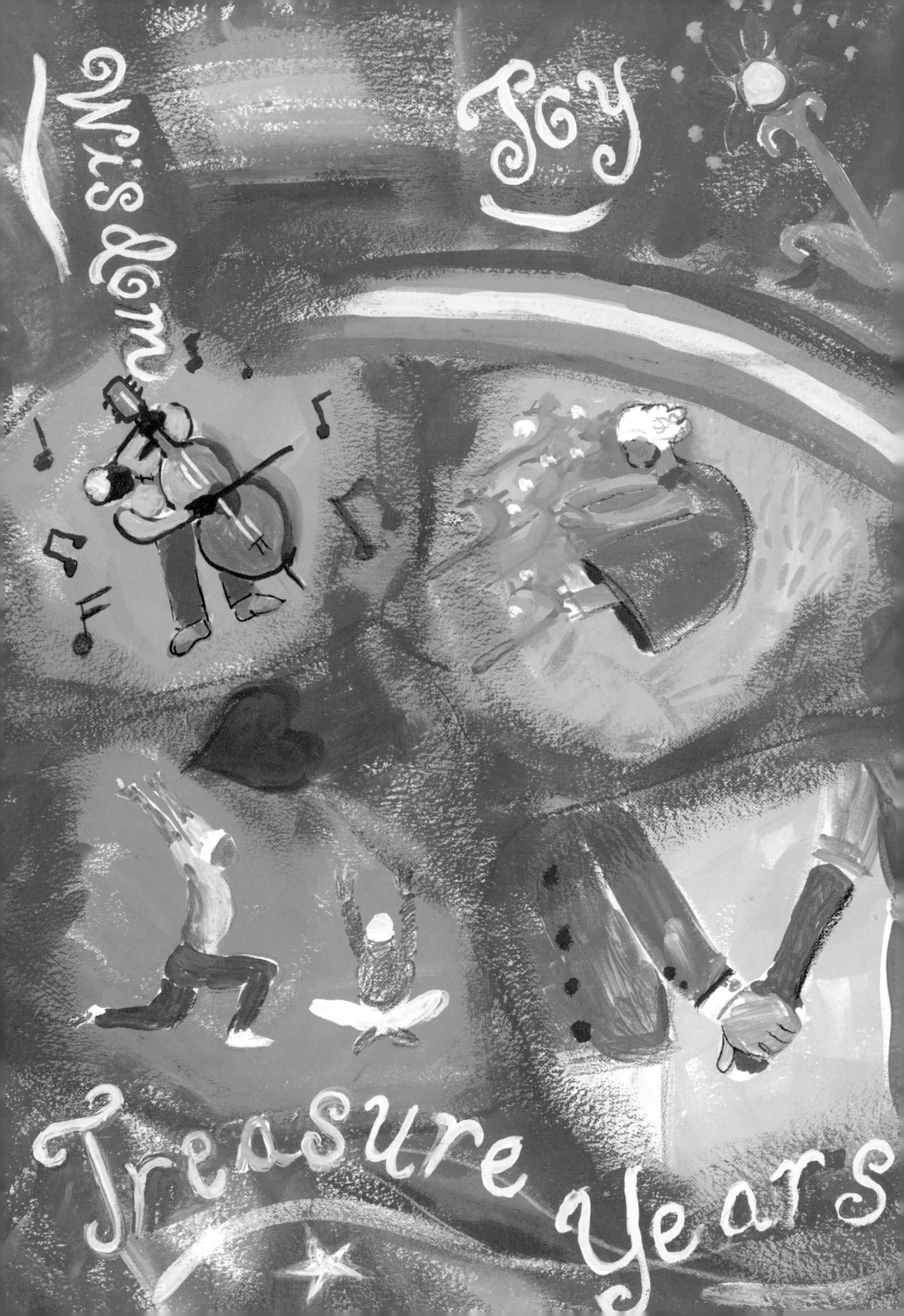
Wisdom
Joy
Treasure Years

Chapter Thirteen

AGING

"I am beautiful and empowered at every age."

Aging Checklist

- [ ] I'm afraid of getting old.
- [ ] I'm scared I'll get wrinkled and fat.
- [ ] I don't want to end up in a nursing home.
- [ ] Being old means I'll be ugly and unwanted.
- [ ] Being old means being sick.
- [ ] No one wants to be around an old person.

No matter what age we are, we will all grow older. We will also have great control over *how* we shall age.

What are the things that age us? Certain beliefs about aging, such as the belief that we have to get sick when we get old. The belief in dis-ease. Hating the body. Believing in a lack of time. Anger and hatred. Self-hatred. Bitterness. Shame and guilt. Fear. Prejudice. Self-righteousness. Being judgmental. Carrying burdens. Giving up our control to others. These are all beliefs that age us.

What do you personally believe about aging? Do you look around at the frail and ill and assume that you'll be that way, too? Do you see the poverty we create among the aging and think that that's your destiny as well? Do you notice how lonely many older people are and fear your own aloneness? We don't have to accept these negative concepts. We can turn all of this around. It doesn't have to continue to be this way. We can take our power back.

Feeling vital and energetic is much more important than a line or two or even more, yet we've agreed that unless we're young and beautiful, we're not acceptable. Why would we agree to such a belief? Where did we lose our love and compassion for ourselves and for each other? We've made living in our bodies an uncomfortable experience. Each day we look for something that's wrong with us, and we worry about every wrinkle. This only makes us feel bad and creates *more* wrinkles. This isn't self-love. This is self-hatred, and it only contributes to our lack of self-esteem.

What are you teaching your children about aging? What is the example you're giving them? Do they see a dynamic, loving person, enjoying each day and looking forward to the future? Or are you a bitter, frightened person, dreading your elder years and expecting to be sick and alone? *Our children learn from us!* And so do our grandchildren. What kind of elder years do we want to help them envision and create?

We used to live very short lives—first only till our mid-teens, then our 20s, then our 30s, then our 40s. Even at the turn of the century, it was considered old to be 50. In 1900, our life expectancy was 47 years. Now we're accepting 80 as a normal life span. Why can't we take a quantum leap in consciousness and make the new level of acceptance 120 or 150 years?!

It's not out of our reach. I see living much longer becoming normal and natural for most of us in a generation or two. Forty-five used to be middle-aged, but that won't be true anymore. I see 75 becoming the new middle age. For generations, we've allowed the numbers that correspond to how many years we've been on the planet to tell us how to feel and how to behave. As with any other aspect of life, what we mentally accept and believe about aging becomes true for us. Well, it's time to change our beliefs about aging! When I look around and see frail, sick, frightened older people, I say to myself, "It doesn't have to be that way." Many of us have learned that by changing our thinking, we can change our lives.

I know we can change our beliefs about aging and make the aging process a positive, vibrant, healthy experience.

We can change our belief systems. But in order to do so, we "Elders of Excellence" need to *get out of the victim mentality*. As long as we see ourselves as being hapless, powerless individuals; as long as we depend on the government to "fix" things for us, we'll never progress as a group. However, when we band together and come up with creative solutions for our later years, then we have real power, and we can change our nation and our world for the better.

It's time for our elders to take back their power from the medical and pharmaceutical industries. They're being buffeted about by high-tech medicine, which is very expensive and destroys their health. It's time for all of us (and especially the elders) to learn to take control of our own health. We need to learn about the body-mind connection—to know that what we do, say, and think contributes to either dis-ease or vibrant health.

EXERCISE: YOUR BELIEFS ABOUT AGING

Answer the following questions as best you can.

1. **How are your parents aging? (Or how *did* they age if they've passed away?)**

_____

_____

_____

_____

_____

_____

2. How old do you feel?

    _____

    _____

    _____

    _____

    _____

    _____

3. What are you doing to help our society/country/planet?

    _____

    _____

    _____

    _____

    _____

    _____

4. How do you create love in your life?

_____

_____

_____

_____

_____

_____

5. Who are your positive role models?

_____

_____

_____

_____

_____

_____

6. What are you teaching your children about aging?

_____

_____

_____

_____

_____

7. What are you doing *today* to prepare for healthy, happy, vital elder years?

_____

_____

_____

_____

_____

8. How do you feel about and treat older people now?

_____

_____

_____

_____

_____

9. How do you envision your life when you're 60, 75, 85?

_____

_____

_____

_____

_____

10. How do you want to be treated when you're older?

_____

_____

_____

_____

_____

_____

11. How do you want to die?

_____

_____

_____

_____

_____

_____

Now go back and mentally turn each negative answer above into a positive affirmation. Know that your later years can be the best years of your life.

❀ ❀ ❀

There's a pot of gold at the end of this rainbow. We know the treasures are there. The later years of our life are to be the years of our greatest treasures. We must learn how to make these the best years of our lives. We learn these secrets later in life. These are secrets to be shared with the generations coming up. (The book *New Cells, New Bodies, New Lives* by Virginia Essene gives us new ideas to think about.)

I know that what I call "youthening" can be done; it's just a matter of finding out how.

Some of the secrets of "youthening":

- Release the word *old* from our vocabulary.
- Turn "aging" into "living longer."
- Be willing to accept new concepts.
- Take a quantum leap in thinking.
- Change life expectancy to 120/150.
- Change our beliefs.
- Reject manipulation.
- Change what we consider "normal."
- Turn dis-ease into vibrant health.
- Take good care of our bodies.
- Release limiting beliefs.
- Be willing to change our thinking.
- Embrace new ideas.
- Accept the truth about ourselves.
- Give selfless service to our communities.

We want to create a conscious ideal of our later years as the most rewarding phase of our lives. We need to know that our future is always bright no matter what our age. We can do this if we just change our thinking. It's time to dispel the fearful images of old age. It's time to take a quantum leap in our thinking. We need to take the word *old* out of our vocabulary and become a country where the long-lived are still young. We want to see our *later years* become our *treasure years*.

Infinite Love Treatment

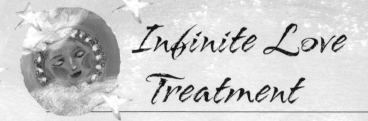

Deep at the center of our being, there is an infinite
well of love, joy, peace, and wisdom. This is true
of each and every one of us. Yet how often do
we get in touch with this treasure within us?
Do we do it once a day? Once in a while? Or do
we totally forget that we have this treasure right
inside of us? Just for a moment, take a deep
breath and connect with that part of yourself.
It only takes a breath to go to your center. You
might close your eyes for a moment and allow
yourself to feel this center within you. Now
consciously go to that infinite well of love within
you. Feel the love that is there. Let it grow and
expand. Then go to that infinite well of joy within
you. Feel the joy. Let it flow.

Healthy Aging Treatment

I am one with Life, and all of Life loves and supports me. Therefore, I claim for myself peace of mind and joy of living for every age of my life. Each day is new and different and brings its own pleasures. I am an active participant in this world. I am an eager student with an intense desire to learn. I take excellent care of my body. I choose thoughts that make me happy. I have a strong spiritual connection that sustains me at all times. I am not my parents, nor do I have to age or die the way they did. I am my own unique self, and I choose to live a deeply fulfilling life until my last day on this planet. I am at peace with living, and I love all of Life. This is the truth of my being, and I accept it as so. All is well in my life.

Part III
YOUR NEW LIFE

Chapter Fourteen

YOUR NEW PICTURE

"I see myself in a new light."

With your nondominant hand (the hand you don't usually use), draw a new picture of yourself. Either use
crayon or ink. Sit quietly. Close your eyes. Breathe. Center
yourself. Meditate on the following questions:

"Who am I?"

"Why am I here?"

"What have I come here to learn?"

"What have I come here to teach?"

"What has changed?"

Picture Yourself Here

What Makes You Happy?

"I recognize that I am the source of my happiness."

Throughout this companion book, we've explored so many areas of our lives. We've uncovered negative patterns and beliefs. We've relinquished old baggage. We feel freer and lighter. We're open and receptive to good. So the next question is: What would make you happy? This is not the time to talk about what you *don't* want. This is a time to be very clear about what you *do* want in your life. List everything that you can think of. Cover all the areas of your life. List at least 50 things.

1. _____

2. _____

3. _____

4. _____

5. _____

6. _____

7. _____

8. _____

9. _____

10. _____

11. _____

12. _____

13. _____

14. _____

15. _____

16. _____

17. _____

18. _____

19. _____

20. _____

21. _____

22. _____

23. _____

24. _____

25. _____

26. _____

27. _____

28. _____

29. _____

30. _____

31. _____

32. _____

33. _____

34. _____

35. _____

36. _____

37. _____

38. _____

39. _____

40. _____

41. _____

42. _____

43. _____

44._____

45._____

46._____

47._____

48._____

49._____

50._____

Now create a positive affirmation for each item. Be aware that anyone who has done as much work as you have in order to change deserves to have a wonderful new world.

1. _____

2. _____

3. _____

4. _____

5. _____

6. _____

7. _____

8. _____

9. _____

10. _____

11. _____

12. _____

13. _____

14. _____

15. _____

16. _____

17. _____

18. _____

19. _____

20. _____

21. _____

22. _____

23. _____

24. _____

25._____

26._____

27._____

28._____

29._____

30._____

31._____

32._____

33._____

34._____

35._____

36._____

37._____

38._____

39._____

40._____

41._____

42. _____

43. _____

44. _____

45. _____

46. _____

47. _____

48. _____

49. _____

50. _____

It's exciting to have wonderful people, places, and things in our lives. However, we must be clear that these things do not "make" us happy. Only *we* can do that. Only we can think the thoughts that create peace and joy. Never give power to an outside person or source. Make yourself happy, and all good will flow to you in abundance.

Mirror Work

Look into the mirror. Breathe. Smile. Say: *"I deserve to have a wonderful life."* Breathe again. Say: *"I deserve everything on my list."* Breathe. Say: *"I deserve and accept all good in my life."* Breathe. Say: *"I am a loving, worthwhile person, and I love myself."* Breathe. Say: *"All is well in my world."*

Each day, you can look into the mirror and say the following:

"I love you, (insert your name). I really, really love you."

"You are my best friend, and I enjoy living my life with you."

"Experiences come and go; however, my love for you is constant. We have a good life together, and it will only get better and better."

"We have many wonderful adventures ahead of us and a life filled with love."

"All the love in our lives begins with us. I love you. I really love you!"

Your New Story

"I see myself in a new light."

Now that you have a list of all the people, things, and situations you would like to have in your life—all of which could contribute to your happiness, let's put them into a story. Write as much or as little as you wish.

I, _____, now have a wonderful life. . . .

_____

_____

_____

_____

_____

_____

_____

_____

_____

_____

_____

_____

_____

_____

_____

_____

_____

_____

_____

_____

_____

_____

_____

Visualization

Now that you've written your new story, see yourself living it. What does your new life feel like? What do you look like as you grow older? See your harmonious relationships. Breathe in your newfound freedom and happiness.

Relaxation and Meditation

Relaxation is essential to the healing process. It's hard to allow the healing energies to flow within us if we're tense and frightened. Dr. Bernie Siegel says, "The physical benefits of mediation have been well documented. It tends to lower or normalize blood pressure, pulse rate, and the level of stress hormones in the blood. Its benefits are also multiplied when combined with regular exercise. In short, it reduces wear and tear on both body and mind, helping people live better and longer."

It only takes a moment or two, several times a day, to allow the body to let go and relax. At any moment, you can close your eyes and take two or three deep breaths and release whatever tension you may be carrying. If you have more time, sit or lie down quietly, and talk your body into complete relaxation. Say silently to yourself: "My toes are relaxing, my feet are relaxing, my ankles are letting go," and so on, working all the way down your body. Or, you may begin with your head and work down.

At the end of this simple exercise, you'll feel peaceful and calm for a while. Repeating this process on a regular basis can create a peaceful state within you. This is a very positive, physical meditation that you can do anywhere.

As a society, we've made meditation into something mysterious and difficult to achieve, yet meditation is one of the oldest and simplest processes we can do. Yes, we can make it complicated with specialized breathing and ritualized mantras. Those meditations are fine for advanced students. Still, everyone can meditate now; it's easy.

All we have to do is to sit or lie down quietly, close our eyes, and take a few deep breaths. The body will automatically relax; we don't have to do anything to force it. We can repeat the words *healing* or *peace* or *love*, or anything that's meaningful to us. We could even say, "I love myself" or "All is well. Everything is working out for my highest good. Out of this situation only good will come. I am safe." We can say silently, "What is it I need to know?" or "I am willing to learn." Then just be there quietly.

Answers may come immediately or in a day or two. Don't feel rushed. Allow things to unfold naturally. Remember that it's the nature of the mind to think; you will never completely rid yourself of dashing thoughts. Allow them to flow. You might notice, "Oh, now I'm thinking fear thoughts or anger thoughts or disaster thoughts or whatever." Don't give these thoughts importance; just let them pass through your mind like soft clouds on a summer sky.

Some say that uncrossing your legs and arms and sitting upright with a straight spine will improve the quality of the meditation. Maybe so. Do it if you can. What's important is to meditate on a regular basis. The practice of meditation is cumulative: The more regularly you do it, the more your body and mind respond to the benefits of relaxation—and the quicker you may get your answers.

Another easy method of meditation is to simply count your breaths as you sit quietly with your eyes closed. Count "one" on the inhale, "two" on the exhale, "three" on the inhale, and so on, counting your breath from one to ten. When you exhale on ten, just begin again at one. If your mind wanders and you find yourself counting up to 18 or 30, merely bring yourself back to one. If you find that you're fretting about your doctor or your job or your kids or about making a shopping list, simply bring yourself back to the count of one.

You can't meditate incorrectly. Any starting point is perfect for you. You can find books that will teach you several methods. You can also find classes that will give you the experience of meditating with others. Begin anywhere. Allow meditation to become a habit.

If you're new to meditation, I would suggest that you begin with only five minutes at a time. People who immediately do 20 or 30 minutes can get bored and skip it entirely. Five minutes once or twice a day is a good beginning. If you can do it at the same time every day, the body begins to look forward to it. Meditation gives you small periods of rest that are beneficial to the healing of your emotions and body.

You see, we all have tremendous wisdom within us. We have all the answers to all the questions we shall ever ask inside of us.

You have no idea how wise you are. You *can* take care of yourself. You *do* have the answers you need. Get connected. You will feel safer and more powerful.

"Know that my support is always with you. I love you."

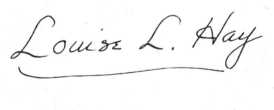

Closing Treatment

I am one with Life, and all of Life loves me
and supports me. The past is over and done.
It has gone back to the nothingness from whence
it came. I am free. I have a new sense of pride
and self-worth. I am confident in my abilities
to love and support myself. I have learned that
I am capable of positive growth and change. I am
strong. I am united with all of life. I am one with
the Universal power and intelligence. Divine
wisdom leads me and guides me every step of the
way. I am safe and secure as I move forward to
my highest good. I do this with ease and joy. I
am a new person, living in a world of my own
choosing. I am deeply grateful for all that I have
and for all that I am. I am blessed and prosperous
in every way. This is the truth of my being, and
I accept it as so. All is well in my world.

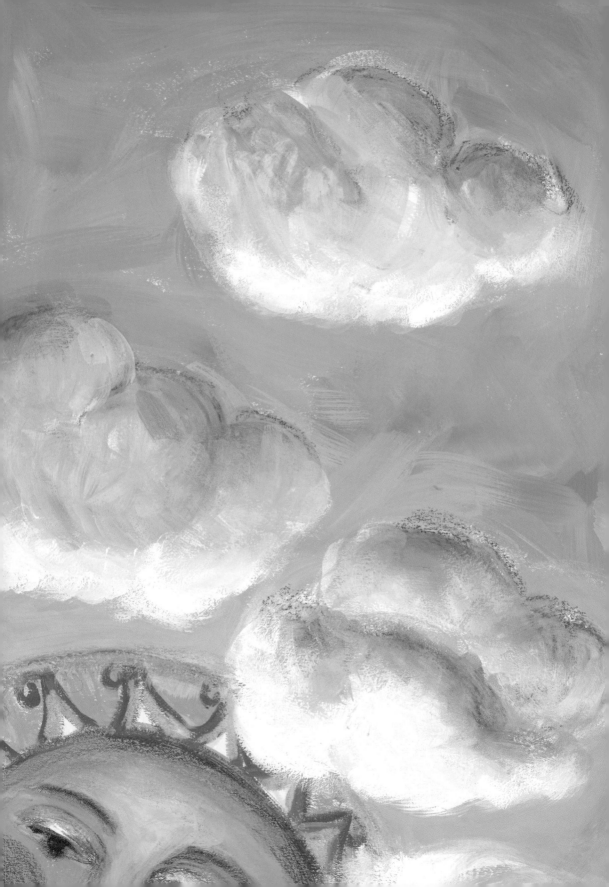

Recommended Reading

Ageless Body, Timeless Mind, by Deepak Chopra, M.D.

Cooking for Healthy Healing, by Linda Rector-Page, N.D., Ph.D.

Do What You Love, the Money Will Follow, by Marsha Sinetar

Everyday Wisdom, by Dr. Wayne W. Dyer

Feel the Fear and Do It Anyway, by Susan Jeffers, Ph.D.

Fire in the Soul, by Joan Borysenko, Ph.D.

Get Out of My Life, But First Could You Drive Me and Cheryl to the Mall: A Parent's Guide to the New Teenager, by Anthony E. Wolf

A God Who Looks Like Me, by Patricia Reilly

Guide to Intuitive Healing, by Judith Orloff, M.D.

Healthy Healing—a Guide to Self-Healing for Everyone, by Linda Rector-Page, Ph.D.

Instead of Therapy: Help Yourself Change and Change the Help You're Getting, by Tom Rusk, M.D.

Life After Life, by Raymond Moody, M.D.

Lifegoals, by Amy E. Dean

Losing Your Pounds of Pain: Breaking the Link Between Abuse, Stress, and Overeating, by Doreen Virtue, Ph.D.

Love, Medicine & Miracles, by Bernie Siegel, M.D.

The Menopause Industry: How the Medical Establishment Exploits Women, by Sandra Coney

Minding the Body, Mending the Mind, by Joan Borysenko, Ph.D.

New Passages, by Gail Sheehy

Opening Our Hearts to Men, by Susan Jeffers, Ph.D.

Real Magic, by Dr. Wayne W. Dyer

The Reconnection, by Dr. Eric Pearl

The Relaxation Response, by Benson and Klipper

A Return to Love, by Marianne Williamson

The Science of Mind, by Ernest Holmes

Self-Parenting, by John Pollard III

Soul Searching (A Girl's Guide to Finding Herself, by Sarah Stillman (age 16)—"Very good!" says Louise

Staying on the Path, by Dr. Wayne W. Dyer

Super Nutrition Gardening, by Dr. William S. Peavy and Warren Peary

The Ten Gifts, by Robin Landew Silverman

Venus in Blue Jeans, by Nathalie Bartle

What Do You Really Want for Your Children, by Dr. Wayne W. Dyer

What Every Woman Needs to Know Before (and After) She Gets Involved with Men and Money, by Judge Lois Forer

When 9 to 5 Isn't Enough, by Marcia Perkins-Reed

The Wisdom of Menopause, by Christiane Northrup, M.D.

A Woman's Worth, by Marianne Williamson

Women's Bodies, Women's Wisdom, by Christiane Northrup, M.D.

Women Who Love Too Much, by Robin Norwood

Your Handwriting Can Change Your Life, by Vimala Rodgers

Your Sacred Self, by Dr. Wayne W. Dyer

Any book by Emmet Fox or Dr. John MacDonald

Also, the audiocassette program, *Making Relationships Work,* by Barbara De Angelis, Ph.D.

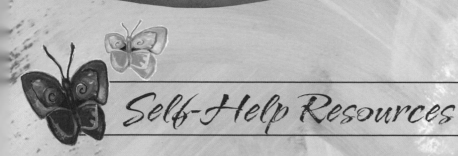

Self-Help Resources

The following list of resources can be used to access information on a variety of issues. The addresses and telephone numbers listed are for the national headquarters; look in your local yellow pages under "Community Services" for resources closer to your area.

In addition to the following groups, other self-help organizations may be available in your area to assist your healing and recovery for a particular life crisis not listed here. Consult your telephone directory, call a counseling center or help line near you, or contact:

AIDS

CBC National AIDS Hotline
(800) 342-2437

Children with AIDS (CWA)
Project of America
(800) 866-AIDS
(24-hour hotline)

The Names Project—
AIDS Quilt
(800) 872-6263

Project Inform
19655 Market St., Ste. 220
San Francisco, CA 94103
(415) 558-8669

PWA Coalition
50 W. 17th St.
New York, NY 10011

Spanish HIV/STD/AIDS
Hotline
(800) 344-7432

TTY (Hearing Impaired)
AIDS Hotline (CDC National
HIV/AIDS)
(800) 243-7889

ALCOHOL ABUSE

Al-Anon Family
Headquarters
1600 Corporate
Landing Parkway

Virginia Beach, VA
23454-5617
(800) 4AL-ANON

Alcoholics
Anonymous (AA)
General Service Office
475 Riverside Dr.
New York, NY 10115
(212) 870-3400

Children of Alcoholics
Foundation
164 W. 74th St.
New York, NY 10023
(800) 359-COAF

Meridian Council, Inc.
Administrative Offices
4 Elmcrest Terrace
Norwalk, CT 06850

Mothers Against Drunk
Driving (MADD)
(254) 690-6233

National Association of Children of Alcoholics (NACOA)
11426 Rockville Pike, Ste. 100
Rockville, MD 20852
(301) 468-0985
(888) 554-2627

National Clearinghouse
for Alcohol and Drug
Information (NCADI)

P.O. Box 234
Rockville, MD 20852
(301) 468-2600

National Council on
Alcoholism and Drug
Dependence (NCADD)
12 West 21st St.
New York, NY 10010
(212) 206-6770
(800) 475-HOPE

Women for Sobriety
(800) 333-1606

ALZHEIMER'S DISEASE

Alzheimer's Association
919 N. Michigan Ave.,
Ste. 1100
Chicago, IL 60611
(800) 621-0379
www.alz.org

Alzheimer's Disease Educa-
tion and Referral Center
P.O. Box 8250
Silver Spring, MD 20907
(800) 438-4380
adear@alzheimers.org

Eldercare Locator
927 15th St. NW, 6th Fl.
Washington, DC 20005
(800) 677-1116

CANCER

National Cancer Institute
(800) 4-CANCER

CHILDREN'S ISSUES

Child Molestation

Child Help USA/
Child Abuse Hotline
232 East Gish Rd.
San Jose, CA 95112
(800) 422-4453

Prevent Child
Abuse America
200 South Michigan Ave.,
Ste. 17
Chicago, IL 60604
(312) 663-3520

Crisis Intervention

Boy's Town
National Hotline
(800) 448-3000

Children of the Night
P.O. Box 4343
Hollywood, CA 90078
(800) 551-1300

Covenant House Hotline
(800) 999-9999

Kid Save Line
(800) 543-7283

Youth Nineline
(referrals for parents/teens
about drugs, homelessness,
runaways)
(800) 999-9999

Missing Children

Missing Children . . .
HELP Center
410 Ware Blvd., Ste. 710
Tampa, FL 33619
(800) USA-KIDS

National Center for Missing
and Exploited Children
699 Prince St.
Alexandria, VA 22314
(800) 843-5678

Children with
Serious Illnesses
(fulfilling wishes):

Brass Ring Society
National Headquarters
213 N. Washington St.
Snow Hill, MD 21863
(410) 632-4700
(800) 666-WISH

Make-a-Wish Foundation
(800) 332-9474

CO-DEPENDENCY

**Co-Dependents
Anonymous**
(602) 277-7991

DEATH/GRIEVING/SUICIDE

Grief Recovery Institute
P.O. Box 461659
Los Angeles, CA
90046-1659
(323) 650-1234
www/grief-recovery.com

**National Hospice and Pallia-
tive Care Organization**
1700 Diagonal Rd., Ste. 300
Alexandria, VA 22314
(703) 243-5900
www.nhpco.org

**SIDS (Sudden Infant Death
Syndrome) Alliance**
1314 Bedford Ave., Ste. 210
Baltimore, MD 21208

Parents of Murdered Children
(recovering from violent death
of friend or family member)
100 E 8th St., Ste. B41
Cincinnati, OH 45202
(513) 721-5683

Survivors of Suicide
Call your local Mental Health

Association for the branch
nearest you.

**AARP Grief
and Loss Programs**
(202) 434-2260
(800) 424-3410 ext. 2260

DEBTS

Credit Referral
(information on local credit
counseling services)
(800) 388-CCCS

Debtors Anonymous
General Service Board
P.O. Box 888
Needham, MA 02492-0009
(781) 453-2743
www.debtorsanonymous.org

DIABETES

**American Diabetes
Association**
(800) 232-3472

DOMESTIC VIOLENCE

**National Coalition Against
Domestic Violence**
P.O. Box 34103
Washington, DC 20043-4103
(202) 745-1211

National Domestic Violence Hotline

P.O. Box 161810
Austin, TX 78716
(800) 799-SAFE

DRUG ABUSE

Cocaine Anonymous National Referral Line
(800) 347-8998

National Helpline of Phoenix House
(cocaine abuse hotline)
(800) 262-2463
(800) COCAINE
www.drughelp.org

National Institute of Drug Abuse (NIDA)
6001 Executive Blvd., Rm. 5213
Bethesda, MD 20892-9561
Parklawn Building
(301) 443-6245
(for information)
(800) 662-4357 (for help)

World Service Office, Inc. (CA)
3740 Overland Ave., Ste. C
Los Angeles, CA
90034-6337
(310) 559-5833
(800) 347-8998
(to leave message)

EATING DISORDERS

Overeaters Anonymous
National Office
P.O. Box 44020
Rio Rancho, NM
87174-4020
(505) 891-2664

GAMBLING

Gamblers Anonymous
New York Intergroup
P.O. Box 7
New York, NY 10116-0007
(212) 903-4400

HEALTH ISSUES

Alzheimer's Association
919 N. Michigan Ave., Ste. 1100
Chicago, IL 60611-1676
(800) 621-0379

American Chronic Pain Association
P.O. Box 850
Rocklin, CA 95677
(916) 632-0922
www.theacpa.org

American Foundation of Traditional Chinese Medicine
P.O. Box 330267
San Francisco, CA 94133
(415) 392-7002

American Holistic
Health Association
P.O. Box 17400
Anaheim, CA 92817
(714) 779-6152
e-mail: ahha.org
www.ahha@healthy.net

Office of Deepak Chopra
The Chopra Center at
La Costa Resort and Spa
2013 Costa Del Mar
Carlsbad, CA 92009
(888) 424-6772
www.chopra.com

The Fetzer Institute
9292 West KL Ave.
Kalamazoo, MI 49009
(616) 375-2000

Hippocrates Health Institute
(a favorite annual
retreat for Louise)
1443 Palmdale Court
West Palm Beach, FL 33411

Hospicelink
190 Westbrook Rd.
Essex, CN 06426
(800) 331-1620

Institute for
Noetic Sciences
P.O. Box 909
Sausalito, CA 94966
(415) 331-5650

The Mind-Body
Medical Institute
110 Francis St., Ste. 1A
Boston, MA 02215
(617) 632-9525

National Health
Information Center
P.O. Box 1133
Washington, DC 20013-1133
(800) 336-4797

Optimum Health
Care Institute
(Louise loves it here!)
6970 Central Ave.
Lemon Grove, CA 91945
(619) 464-3346

Preventive Medicine
Research Institute
Dean Ornish, M.D.
900 Bridgeway, Ste. 2
Sausalito, CA 94965
(415) 332-2525

HOUSING RESOURCES

Acorn
(nonprofit network of low- and
moderate-income housing)
739 8th St., S.E.
Washington, DC 20003
(202) 547-9292

IMPOTENCE

**Impotence Institute
of America**
P.O. Box 410
Bowie, MD 20718-0410
(800) 669-1603
www.impotenceworld.org

MENTAL HEALTH

**American Psychiatric
Association of America**
www.psych.org

**Anxiety Disorders
Association of America**
www.adaa.org

**The Help Center of the
American Psychological
Association**
www.helping.apa.org

**The International Society for
Mental Health Online**
www.ismho.org

**Knowledge
Exchange Network**
www.mentalhealth.org

**National Center for Post-
Traumatic Stress Disorder
(PTSD)**
www.dartmouth.edu/dms/ptsd

**National Alliance for the
Mentally Ill**
www.nami.org

**National Depressive and
Manic-Depressive Association**
www.ndM.D.a.org

**National Institute of
Mental Health**
www.nimh.nih.gov

PET BEREAVEMENT

Bide-A-Wee Foundation
410 E. 38th St.
New York, NY 10016
(212) 532-6395

**Holistic Animal
Consulting Centre**
29 Lyman Ave.
Staten Island, NY 10305
(718) 720-5548

RAPE/SEXUAL ISSUES

**Rape, Abuse, and Incest
National Network**
(800) 656-4673

Safe Place
P.O. Box 19454
Austin, TX 78760
(512) 440-7273

National Council on Sexual Addictions and Compulsivity
1090 S. Northchase Parkway, Ste. 200
South Marietta, GA 30067
(770) 989-9754

Sexually Transmitted Disease Referral
(800) 227-8922

SMOKING

Nicotine Anonymous
P.O. Box 126338
Harrisburg, PA 17112
(415) 750-0328
www.nicotine-anonymous.org

STRESS REDUCTION

The Biofeedback & Psychophysiology Clinic
The Menninger Clinic
P.O. Box 829
Topeka, KS 66601-0829
(913) 350-5000

New York Open Center
(In-depth workshops to invigorate the spirit)
83 Spring St.
New York, NY 10012
(212) 219-2527

Omega Institute
(a healing, spiritual retreat community)
150 Lake Dr.
Rhinebeck, NY 12572-3212
(845) 266-4444 (info)
(800) 944-1001 (to enroll)

The Stress Reduction Clinic
Center for Mindfulness
University of Massachusetts
Medical Center
55 Lake Ave. North
Worcester, MA 01655
(508) 856-1616
(508) 856-2656

TEEN HELP

ADOL: Adolescent Directory Online
Includes information on eating disorders, depression, and teen pregnancy.
www.education.indiana.edu/cas/adol/adol.html

Al-Anon/Alateen
1600 Corporate
Landing Parkway
Virginia Beach, VA 23454-5617
(888) 425-2666
(888) 4AL-ANON
www.al-anon.org

Focus Adolescent Services: Eating Disorders
www.focusas.com/EatingDisorders.html

Future Point
A nonprofit organization that offers message boards and chat rooms to empower teens in the academic world and beyond.
www.futurepoint.org

Kids in Trouble Help Page
Child abuse, depression, suicide, and runaway resources, with links and hotline numbers.
www.geocities.com/EnchantedForest/2910

Planned Parenthood
810 Seventh Ave.
New York, NY 10019
(212) 541-7800
www.plannedparenthood.org

SafeTeens.com
Provides lessons on online safety and privacy; also has resources for homework and fun on the web.
www.safeteens.com

TeenCentral.net
This site is written by and about teens. Includes celebrity stories, real-teen tales, an anonymous help-line, and crisis counseling.
www.teencentral.net

TeenOutReach.com
Includes all kinds of information geared at teens, from sports to entertainment to help with drugs and eating disorders.
www.teenoutreach.com

Hotlines for Teenagers

Boys Town National Hotline
(800) 448-3000

Childhelp National Child Abuse Hotline/ Voices for Children
(800) 422-4453
(800) 4ACHILD

Just for Kids Hotline
(888) 594-5437
(888) 594-KIDS

National Child Abuse Hotline
(800) 792-5200

National Runaway Hotline
(800) 621-4000

National Youth Crisis Hotline
(800) 442-4673
(800) 442-HOPE

Suicide Prevention Hotline
(800) 827-7571

© 1999 Charles William Bush Photography

About the Author

Louise L. Hay is a metaphysical lecturer and teacher and the bestselling author of numerous books, including *You Can Heal Your Life* and *Empowering Women*. Her works have been translated into 25 different languages in 33 countries throughout the world. Since beginning her career as a Science of Mind minister in 1981, Louise has assisted millions of people in discovering and using the full potential of their own creative powers for personal growth and self-healing. Louise is the owner and founder of Hay House, Inc., a publishing company that disseminates books, audios, and videos that contribute to the healing of the planet.

Websites: **www.LouiseHay.com** or **www.LouiseLHay.com**

Other Selected Hay House Lifestyles Titles

Books

Aromatherapy A–Z, by Connie Higley, Alan Higley, and Pat Leatham

Aromatherapy 101, by Karen Downes

Dream Journal, by Leon Nacson

Healing with Herbs and Home Remedies A–Z, by Hanna Kroeger

Home Design with Feng Shui A–Z, by Terah Kathryn Collins

Homeopathy A–Z, by Dana Ullman, M.P.H.

Inner Wisdom, by Louise L. Hay

Interpreting Dreams A–Z, by Leon Nacson

A Journal of Love and Healing,
by Sylvia Browne and Nancy Dufresne

The Love and Power Journal, by Lynn V. Andrews

Meditations, by Sylvia Browne

Natural Healing for Dogs and Cats A–Z, by Cheryl Schwartz, D.V.M.

Natural Pregnancy A–Z, by Carolle Jean-Murat, M.D.

Pleasant Dreams, by Amy E. Dean

Prayers, by Sylvia Browne

Space Clearing A–Z, by Denise Linn

What Color Is Your Personality?, by Carol Ritberger, Ph.D.

Card Decks

Feng Shui Personal Paradise Cards (booklet and card pack),
by Terah Kathryn Collins

The Four Agreements, by DON Miguel Ruiz

Healing with the Angels Oracle Cards (booklet and card pack),
by Doreen Virtue, Ph.D.

Healing with the Fairies Oracle Cards (booklet and card pack),
by Doreen Virtue, Ph.D.

Heart and Soul, by Sylvia Browne

If Life Is a Game, These Are the Rules Cards,
by Chérie Carter-Scott, Ph.D.

Inner Peace Cards, by Dr. Wayne W. Dyer

MarsVenus Cards, by John Gray

Messages from Your Angels Oracle Cards, by Doreen Virtue, Ph.D.

Miracle Cards, by Marianne Williamson

Money Cards, by Suze Orman

Self-Care Cards, by Cheryl Richardson

Zen Cards, by Daniel Levin

All of the above titles may be ordered by calling
Hay House at the numbers on the next page.

We hope you enjoyed this Hay House book. If you'd like to receive a free catalog featuring additional Hay House books and products, or if you'd like information about the Hay Foundation, please contact:

Hay House, Inc.
P.O. Box 5100
Carlsbad, CA 92018-5100

(760) 431-7695 or **(800) 654-5126**
(760) 431-6948 (fax) or **(800) 650-5115 (fax)**
www.hayhouse.com® • **www.hayfoundation.org**

Published and distributed in Australia by: Hay House Australia Pty. Ltd.,
18/36 Ralph St., Alexandria NSW 2015 • *Phone:* 612-9669-4299
Fax: 612-9669-4144 • www.hayhouse.com.au

Published and distributed in the United Kingdom by: Hay House UK, Ltd., 292B Kensal Rd.,
London W10 5BE • *Phone:* 44-20-8962-1230 • *Fax:* 44-20-8962-1239 • www.hayhouse.co.uk

Published and distributed in the Republic of South Africa by: Hay House SA (Pty), Ltd.,
P.O. Box 990, Witkoppen 2068 • *Phone/Fax:* 27-11-706-6612 • orders@psdprom.co.za

Published in India by: Hay House Publications (India) Pvt. Ltd.,
Muskaan Complex, Plot No. 3, B-2, Vasant Kunj, New Delhi 110 070
Phone: 91-11-4176-1620 • *Fax:* 91-11-4176-1630 • www.hayhouseindia.co.in

Distributed in Canada by: Raincoast, 9050 Shaughnessy St., Vancouver, B.C. V6P 6E5
Phone: (604) 323-7100 • *Fax:* (604) 323-2600 • www.raincoast.com

Tune in to **HayHouseRadio.com®** for the best in inspirational talk radio featuring top Hay House authors! And, sign up via the Hay House USA Website to receive the Hay House online newsletter and stay informed about what's going on with your favorite authors. You'll receive bimonthly announcements about Discounts and Offers, Special Events, Product Highlights, Free Excerpts, Giveaways, and more!
www.hayhouse.com®

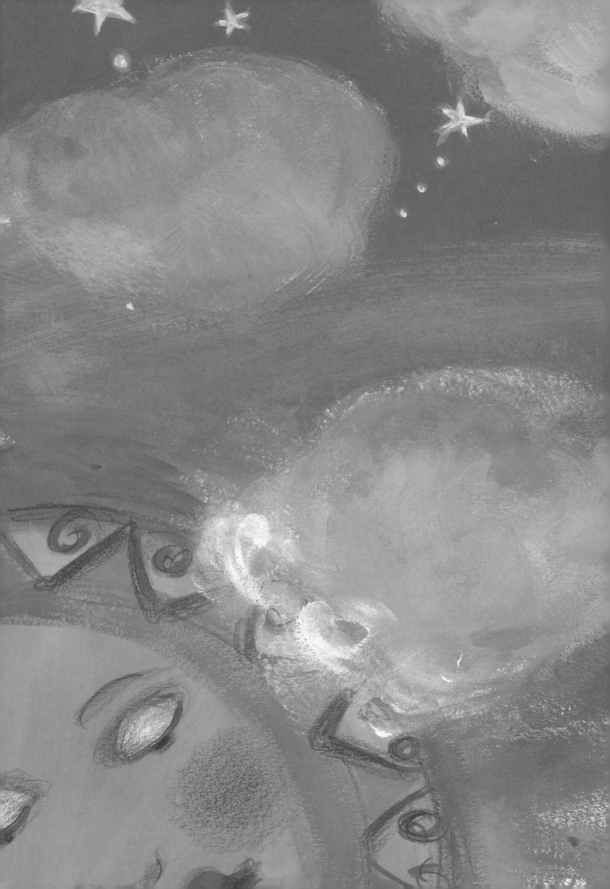